MW00609941

Grandpa Glen's Story

The Saga of a Baby-Boomer

by Glen Van Antwerp

DECEMBER 2019

ISBN: 978-1-64786-848-2

COVER: PHOTO BY GLEN VAN ANTWERP

PUBLISHER

CADILLAC PRINTING COMPANY, INC.

CADILLAC, MICHIGAN 49601

(231) 775-2488

orders@cadillacprintingco.com

This story is dedicated to Glen's grandchildren:

Lydia, James, Rebekah, Margaret, Bronwyn, John, Iain, Helen, and Elizabeth.

Glen's eight oldest grandchildren come in cousin pairs. As of 2020, the oldest pair are college students. The next ones are in high school. They are followed by a pair of middle-schoolers and a pair of elementary students. A tag-along preschooler wraps up the bunch.

Glen hopes that his grandchildren, along with other readers, find this book interesting throughout their lives.

Dear Grandkids,

This memoir of my life wasn't a memoir when I started. I wanted to tell about Sam the crow, my beloved pet. But a scary diagnosis of cancer pushed me to tell more about the lifetime that made me who I am, and made you who you are, too—at least in part.

The story starts with small towns. My parents, your great-grandparents, were descended from farmers who lived in northwest lower Michigan. They knew the deprivations—and the joys—of farming and small-town life. They also knew the pitiless challenges of a worldwide depression and a second world war. With hard work and intelligence, my parents eventually became prosperous, but it was a long struggle.

I love history, but I see it as complicated. Empires, nations, families, and individuals are all a mix of good and bad—wheat and tares growing together. I'll attempt to paint a balanced picture.

I'll get to Sam, my crow, soon. But let's start back on those farms where my folks grew up. Considering the troubles in the world and the difficulties of farm life, my parents had a happy and prosperous start to their adult lives, into which I, or at least my birth, inadvertently brought a good deal of trouble.

Love, Grandpa Glen

Glen's parents at their wedding.

Chapter 1 – Before Hudsonville

My parents, Stan and Margaret, were born on farms in Osceola County, Michigan—my dad near Tustin and my mom close to Ashton. They grew up fifteen miles apart but didn't know each other. They met at a young people's event at a Tustin church after high school. They became friends, just friends, as they double-dated in opposite couples.

My mother graduated at the top of her class from Reed City High School. She dreamed of going to college and didn't think it unreasonable. Several of her mother's brothers and sisters were college graduates. However, the Great Depression of the 1930s still cast its long shadow, and Margaret's family had no extra money. Margaret needed encouragement and scholarship recommendations. Her high school principal offered neither. He thought that sending a farm girl to college was a waste, even if she was valedictorian.

Back then, townspeople were a higher class than country people. There was no point in sending a country girl to college. Even if she graduated, she would likely marry an ignorant farmer and do nothing with her degree. It was better to save college aid for those who would really use it. My mother was not deterred. She got a factory job in Cadillac twenty-five miles away, and moved to a boarding house. After a year or two of scrimping and saving, with a loan from her Aunt Lily, she started college.

Lily didn't think it a waste to send a farm girl to college. She herself was proof of that. Her farm upbringing didn't stop her from earning a graduate degree and becoming a college professor. With Lily's help and encouragement, my mother enrolled at Ferris Institute in Big Rapids, Michigan. She quickly excelled in her business courses.

Meanwhile, my dad (also a farm kid and by no means valedictorian) moved to Grand Rapids, Michigan, for factory work. By this time, the United States had entered World War II, and he was about to be drafted. Stan joined the Navy where he spent almost two years on a gasoline tanker in the Mediterranean Sea.

 Margaret was also called to wartime service in a different way. The War Department, needing secretaries, sent recruiters to business schools across the country. They persuaded promising students to leave their studies for immediate work in Washington, D.C. My mother became secretary to an Army Colonel, a gentleman from an old and wealthy Virginia family. It was a different world for a Michigan farm girl.

Margaret remembered Stan fondly. She wrote him a letter, he replied, and their correspondence grew steady—a bright spot in their lives. Their letters stayed light and casual, as military censors monitored every back-and-forth note between civilians and troops.

My dad came back to America after Germany's fall and was assigned to a Virginia base near Margaret. He was now training, sometimes near D.C. and also in Chicago, for reassignment to the Pacific Ocean and war with Japan. Everyone expected a long, bitter conflict with massive casualties on both sides. The atomic bomb and an abrupt end to the war would surprise everyone.

Stan contacted Margaret, and they started seeing each other. After just three months of whirlwind courtship, they married. When the war ended and my dad was discharged, they moved home to Northern Michigan. Stan planned to use his military training to become a civilian electrician. He hoped to earn a living wiring rural houses. It didn't work out. He couldn't find enough business and was too slow at what work he did.

Congress passed The Serviceman's Readjustment Act (the G.I. Bill) in 1944, providing tax-free college expenses for veterans. Stan jumped at the chance, joining millions of ex-servicemen going to college after the war. He majored in Electrical Engineering at Michigan State College. My mother put her secretarial skills to work, earning money editing and typing student papers. She wrote final copies for many Masters and Doctoral papers, all without her own degree.

She also helped my father with his studies, typed his papers, and even did writing assignments for an English class. He got a "B" as his course grade. She then learned that students were supposed to use a course textbook, something never mentioned or purchased. She could have earned an "A."

My parents lived in a little trailer park near Michigan State named "Trailer Haven." It sat behind Coral Gables off Grand River Avenue, about a mile's walk from campus. Trailer Haven housed a hundred trailers, each on its own little lot with electricity and cold-water hookup. Utility buildings at each end of the park provided toilets, washing machines, showers, and sinks. Every morning saw lineups as residents emptied their nighttime chamber pots.

My parents' trailer, fairly typical in size and layout, was about eight feet wide and sixteen feet long. It had a double bed across the left end as you came in the door, and a dining area at the other end. It held several built-in storage areas and a little kitchenette that ran along the wall opposite the door. A small fuel-oil heater occupied the near wall. Just outside, an attached shed added storage space and a covered entry.

Stan made this trailer himself, starting with elm boards cut and soaked. He bent the boards on a frame, dried them to an arched pattern, and attached them to a trailer chassis. Next, he covered this frame with aluminum outside and varnished plywood inside. The final product looked like a handcrafted Airstream trailer.

Alan and Leah, my dad's brother and his wife, lived in the trailer next to my parents. Alan was a G.I. Bill student too. The Van Antwerp backyards, holding clotheslines and vegetable gardens, bordered a farm across the fence. Both front yards held pretty flower beds. The park owners often showed these lots to demonstrate trailer-park potential.

I conveniently came into the world on a Sunday morning, the only time when my father wasn't busy with full-time studies or part-time employment. At the hospital, the attending doctor was busy elsewhere and my mother waited.

"Don't push," the nurse kept saying, "Wait for the doctor."

My mother tried—tried too hard. The doctor finally arrived, my mother pushed, and I was born blue. Blue from lack of oxygen, darker than an African-American baby born at the same time. "Blue baby syndrome" is dangerous and can cause permanent brain damage. Maybe it did.

I was born into a life different from earlier generations. The Great Depression of the 1930's had given way to a thriving economy. The Amish-like childhoods of my parents were replaced by town jobs and town living. Vaccinations and antibiotics were dramatically improving health. It was an amazing time of new opportunities.

This picture of Ellen standing outside the homemade trailer, was taken before Glen was born.

The following letter was written from my mother to my father when they were first dating.

14 March 1945

Dearest Stan,

Just in from church and found your letter of yesterday noon waiting. Perhaps you'll have left Chi. when this gets there but mebbe not so I'll write anyway. It'll be swell to see you, hon, if only for an hour or a half hour between trains. If it's during the day call me at work and I'll try to get off and grab a cab for the station.

Hope this lovely spring-like weather continues. Wonder how 'tis in Chicago. Had my supper in the Pentagon today and walked from Constitution Ave. to church. Stopped at the photographers as the pictures were to be ready today, only they weren't yet. It was really a pleasure to be walking, tho the pleasure would've been multiplied many times, had you been with me!

Had lots of time so I wrote a long-postponed letter to a girlfriend in nurse's training before time for church. She'll be happy to hear about us cuz she's another who believes firmly that the Lord does truly care for His own. Yes, we'll trust His leading in the days to come, knowing whatever happens it's for the best.

Be seeing you, I hope!!
Lovingly,
Peg

10

Dear Grandkids,

My parents' lives were not easier after my birth.

Eventually, we would have five kids in the family—my older sister Ellen, myself, my brother Bruce, then Ross, and my younger sister Marian. Ellen was not the problem.

Ellen was born three and a half years before I was. She was smart, sunny and helpful. Then my mother gave birth to me, my younger brother, and my youngest brother in another three-and-a-half years. We were loud, active, and wild—quite unlike our charming sister.

During these years, my mother also had a miscarriage and contracted polio. Mounting medical costs caused their medical insurance to be canceled for overuse. Then, in the next six years we moved six times. I can't imagine how hard their lives must have been.

Love Grandpa Glen

Glen and his siblings at the 1st Hudsonville rental.
Left to Right:
Ellen, Glen, Ross, Bruce.

Chapter 2 – Becoming a Hudsonville Kid

My dad graduated and found an engineering job in Reed City, close to both sets of their parents. We lived in an apartment, part of a dilapidated house, on the north edge of town. My sister's one-room schoolhouse was a half-mile's walk away. I got to tag along and visit sometimes, but I wasn't an early bloomer like Ellen. In fact, I didn't even talk until I was three years old— pointing and crowing instead. Ellen hovered and interpreted. My grandmother called me her "little rooster boy."

Stan and Margaret, surrounded by friends and relatives, were happy in Reed City. Then my dad's company relocated to Hudsonville in Ottawa County, Michigan. My parents, chose to keep the job and follow the company. We moved shortly before my fourth birthday.

Hudsonville stood on a patch of high ground carved by a large bend in what had once been a great river. In the course of time, as great rivers often do, it flowed elsewhere and its old path became a swamp. For hundreds and perhaps thousands of years, swamp vegetation grew, died and rotted away. It built a broad bed of rich soil that was eight feet deep but always wet.

The first settlers of European descent founded Hudsonville about a century before I was born. It was a tiny town surrounded by swamp on three sides. Twenty years later, a Grand-Rapids-to-Chicago railway connected Hudsonville to the wider world.

Then, in the 1890s, Dutch immigrants followed the railroad and began settling around Hudsonville. They came from a country that had turned wetlands to farms for a thousand years. They dug drainage ditches and converted swamps into fertile fields. These new farmlands, called "muck fields," were very productive. They were good for growing high-value crops like celery, carrots, and onions—especially onions.

The first Dutchmen in Hudsonville arrived seventy years before my family. They and their descendants thrived. By the time we came, the very-Dutch town was a prosperous community of stores, churches, and produce-packing plants. Everyone seemed to be related to everyone else, somehow. They were fine people, but their lives were full. They didn't need new friends.

It was a major culture shock for my family. We had a Dutch surname, but as descendants of 1600's immigrants, it didn't count in Hudsonville. My mother, more than the rest of us, felt isolated and alone. Years later, my parents had many close friends in Hudsonville, but the first years were lonely ones.

We lived in an apartment at the corner of Main Street and School Street. A grocery store and the Reformed Church sat across the street in one direction and another. My friend and constant companion, Jimmy, lived nearby. Once, when we were playing with toy trucks, he said, "Let's play firemen."

He had a firetruck. I had a fuel delivery truck. I said, "My truck has gas. Gas makes fires. It doesn't put them out." He paused and answered, "Let's start fires and then put them out!" Problem solved!

Sometime later, Jimmy's family moved to downtown Grand Rapids, near Butterworth Hospital. I missed him. My mother arranged a visit. Maybe she had an appointment or errands nearby. She dropped me off and we played outside while Jimmy's mother occasionally checked on us. We took turns riding his tricycle on the sidewalk in front of his house.

My turn on the trike came. I rode all the way to the corner, turned, and kept riding. I happily pedaled another block and turned again. I had come to Michigan Avenue, a big and busy road even then. I happily raced down a long hill. I didn't know that Jimmy's mother was frantically searching for me. Then she ran up, stopped the speeding tricycle, and marched me home. That was the end of visits with Jimmy.

Later, another friend, a boy named Freddy, moved to Grandville—seven miles from Hudsonville. My mother often took me to Freddy's house, where we were always happy to see each other. I am amazed, looking back, that my mother drove me to friends' houses. Those were not times when people, especially my parents, wasted gasoline on frivolous trips. Perhaps her own loneliness highlighted my need for friends.

This was a time when my mother was overwhelmed with sadness and despair. She suffered from low thyroid function, a condition that produces fatigue and depression. The burden of being physically unwell, socially isolated, and financially strained was almost unbearable. The additional stress of managing her wild children was too much. She sank into a depression that went undiagnosed and untreated.

During that time, my mother would sometimes say, "You kids are going to drive me to Kalamazoo." She meant the state psychiatric hospital, but we thought it was a joke. Once, I got her suitcase to start packing, thinking it the best joke of all. My dad, busy with his own work, was neither empathetic nor sympathetic by temperament or training.

The owner and landlord of our Hudsonville apartment was a proper Dutchman. He believed that cleanliness was next to godliness—or maybe beyond it. He was appalled when he came to our apartment one day and found it strewn with toys, dirty clothes, and unmade beds. A pile of unwashed dishes sat in the sink. We boys were tearing around while my sister stood on a chair at the stove, cooking lunch. My mother lay sick in bed. The proper Dutchman was mortified and shortly kicked us out.

My parents found another rental, an old farmhouse out in the country with cold running water in the kitchen and an outhouse in the back yard. We spent a pleasant summer in this simple home playing outdoors, climbing the big grassy hill across the road, and enjoying birds and flowers. Sometimes we walked down the road and bought eggs at the next farm.

Meanwhile, my parents found a home for sale on Spring Street in town. We moved in, our sixth move in six years, and my parents never moved again.

Our family was still paying off medical bills when we purchased our home. My dad was an engineer, but factory workers lived better than we did. My dad's boss asked, "Stan, why are you buying a $7,500 shack instead of a $10,000 house?" It was a reasonable question, but we couldn't really afford a $7,500 shack, let alone a $10,000 house.

My dad's boss called the place a shack, but it was fine for us. The main floor held my parents' bedroom, a living room, kitchen, dining room, and bathroom. Steep, twisty stairs led to two small bedrooms on the second floor. The house was poorly insulated and lacked upstairs heating. Ice formed on our bedroom windows during the winter, but we slept fine under extra layers of quilts.

We moved just before I started kindergarten. I was almost five and Bruce was nearly three. He missed the country house and cried his first night in our new home. I pointed at the railroad curtains in our new bedroom and said, "Bruce, look at the trains."

"See the engine and coal car," I continued. "Wouldn't it be fun to ride in the caboose?"

Bruce loved trains. Focused on our bedroom curtains, he finally fell asleep.

The best part of our house was its setting, both its lot and neighborhood. Several huge maple trees grew near the house. A big garden sat out back. Only one house stood between us and the Christian School yard—a great place for kids to play. In the other direction, past several houses, a creek flowed. Then endless fields and woodlands stretched forever.

I had many playmates in my new neighborhood. Hudsonville was crawling with kids. Our little dead-end

Spring Street held just eight houses. Yet, at least twenty kids lived on our block. This was typical all over town.

Glen (right side) and his siblings at their first Christmas in the Spring Street house.

Dear Grandkids,

My family was rather dysfunctional and odd, at least by Hudsonville standards.

On top of this, my parents had us call them "Momma" and "Daddy." I have no idea where my northern parents adopted these southern terms. It felt peculiar and babyish as we grew older, especially as other kids in town called their parents "Mom" and "Dad."

I called them "Momma and Daddy" when speaking to them but "Mother and Father" or "Mom and Dad" when speaking about them. Is that strange? I still don't know.

Love, Grandpa Glen

Glen's kindergarten class. Glen is in the front row, second from the left, in a cowboy outfit.

Chapter 3—The Old School

I started school soon after moving to Spring Street. Still four years old until my October birthday, I was the youngest kid in class. I couldn't pronounce A's or R's so my teacher, Mrs. Raterink, was "Missus Wuhtuhwink" to me. She was a lovely lady whose pupils adored her.

My class held all twenty-two public-school kindergartners in the district. Thirteen years later, I graduated from high school in a class of 160 students. Our little group had swelled due to school district consolidation, as well as from new people moving in.

Ellen and I walked to school past the Christian school playground, our first Hudsonville home, and a pretty brick house with stained-glass windows. We passed a charming yard with towering pine trees, trim flowerbeds, and a little goldfish pond.

We came to the school, set far back on an extra-large lot. It was actually two buildings joined together—the older one held elementary grades while the other housed junior-high and high school classes. The tiny gym behind the elementary building served all grades and hosted community events.

My kindergarten room was on the top floor of the elementary building. Our ceilings towered ten feet above worn hardwood floors. An outside wall with oak-trimmed windows took one side of the classroom. An old ventilation shaft, with a fireplace-like opening, sat near the door. It had originally led to rooftop vents when coal-fired heating was cheap. It fascinated us. We sometimes crawled in, lay on our backs and stared up.

The temptation of this view was too strong for my friend, Alan. Mrs. Raterink had stepped out of the room saying, "Be good, I'll be back in a minute."

Alan said, "I'm going up."

He braced his hands and feet against opposite sides of the shaft, and scrambled spider-like upwards as I poked my head in to watch. Returning to a scene of great commotion, Mrs. Raterink urgently coaxed Alan down. The custodian soon closed the shaft forever, and I envied Alan for his adventure.

I don't remember learning anything in kindergarten. Although I didn't know ABC's and couldn't count past ten, I loved being with friends. First grade continued like kindergarten. I had fun but didn't learn much.

Our teacher, Mrs. Coates, had a method for teaching reading. First, she read a section of the primer aloud. Then she called on one student and another to read the same section. I couldn't read, but had a good memory. My turn came and I looked intently at the book while reciting, "See Spot run. Run, Spot, run."

A tornado hit our town in April that year. It was a giant storm that still ranks as one of Michigan's largest ever. We were eating supper on a warm spring evening. My chair sat across from a west-facing window that suddenly showed a writhing black column. It looked like a thousand barns ablaze. I pointed and yelled, "Look at that big fire."

"That's no fire," my dad shouted, "Everyone to the basement!"

The storm missed our house by half a mile, but many people, including friends from school and church, were less fortunate. They lost homes, possessions and loved ones. The storm stayed on the ground for many miles and left 360 people killed or injured. After that, living in Hudsonville meant living in fear of tornados.

I finished first grade and was promoted in spite of how little I knew. Then a breakthrough came. My mother read me newspaper comics every day, but one day she refused. "Read them yourself," she insisted.

"I don't know how to read," I whined.

"I'll help you with words, but I won't read for you."

This was motivation! Fooling Mrs. Coates was one thing but going without comics was another. I mastered reading, and my motivation grew as I learned counting and basic math. Ellen helped tutor me. I began to enjoy school for learning as well as social times.

My new best friend was a boy named Bobby who was a year older. His sister Josie and my sister Ellen were sixth-graders and best friends. Bobby and Josie, new to town, were unusual in several ways. First, they were the only kids in their small family. Second, both their parents worked full-time—their father as a Hudsonville High School teacher and their mother as a Grand Rapids police officer. Third, they had an adult-free home to themselves every afternoon.

They lived next to the high school, and Bobby and I loved to play on a big concrete slab there. We pretended we were on a raft, drifting across the Pacific, sole survivors of a sunken ship. We dreamed up endless stories and entertained ourselves for hours.

Ellen and Josie decided on a Christmas pageant. They wrote a script, assigned roles to siblings, conducted rehearsals, and directed the production. My brother Bruce became Rudolph the Red-Nosed Reindeer. The girls created a costume—a red-tipped, brown cone for a face, topped with deer antlers. Rudolph stayed in a stable, a cardboard box with shutters.

We decorated the basement, made props, and learned our parts. Then, we passed out flyers at school, saying our pageant would be a "March of Dimes" benefit. Tickets were ten cents apiece. The older girls publicized the pageant well. We had a full house at performance time including a troublesome bunch of sixth-grade boys. No adults were present.

The pageant started well. We did our best to play our parts. Then the older boys interrupted with jeering and scoffing, especially when Rudolph stuck his head out. The big boys left the audience, came on stage, unmasked our reindeer, and made fun of our sorry play. An indignant audience demanded refunds. They left in disgust. Only a few compassionate kids let us keep their dimes.

We sat down to discuss how to handle the money. Ellen was determined and principled, just like our dad. She insisted that we had advertised as a benefit and couldn't change it. Bobby and Josie reasoned that the play was a flop, there wasn't much money, and we might as well keep something for our trouble.

Eventually we split the dimes fifty-fifty. Bobby and Josie would do what they wanted with theirs and we with ours. My sister marched us straight to the grocery store where we shuffled sadly past the candy, and deposited our coins in a "March of Dimes" donation jar.

Bobby and I liked to play together, but he grew impatient when my little brothers tagged along. Bobby had a BB pistol that resembled his mother's gun. Other kids owned BB rifles, but Bobby was the only one with a pistol.

One time, while we took turns shooting the gun, Bruce hung around begging for a turn. Bobby told him to go away, but Bruce wouldn't leave.

Bobby aimed his pistol at my brother's leg and fired. The BB didn't go through his jeans but still stung. Bruce howled and ran away. I felt bad but Bobby didn't. He was sure he was right. Kids back then solved their own problems in their own way.

Sometime later, and completely unrelated to this incident, Bobby's family moved. I never saw my best friend again.

Dear Grandkids,

Hudsonville's old public-school building held all students K-12 when I started kindergarten. It couldn't stay that way. The school was quickly becoming too small.

Our school board decided to construct two brand-new elementary buildings. The one on the south edge of town would be "South School." The one on the west side, next to Hughes Park, would be "Park School."

Students would be assigned to the school closest to their neighborhood. South Elementary would be mine, but many of my best friends would go to Park.

I always loved having friends at school and would miss those who went elsewhere. I hope you always have friends at school.

Love Grandpa Glen

Park School seen from the outside.
South School had the same layout.

Chapter 4—New School

The new elementary schools were one-story buildings with seven classrooms lined up, side by side. Each room had a small bathroom in back and cement-block walls. The front wall held windows and a door to outside. There were no hallways, no office, no gym. It was a frugal design that suited our Dutch community.

The new schools, built for future growth, would be half full at first. Teachers taught two grades in one room—a first/second split, a third/fourth, and a fifth/sixth. Park School was ready at the beginning of the school year, but South wasn't. Future South students like myself stayed in the old school for a month or two. Then my short, quiet stroll became a one-mile walk that crossed a busy highway and well-used railroad tracks.

The new schoolyard was big and open, about ten or fifteen acres of former fields and rolling hills. Beyond the schoolyard, more fields and woodlands stretched for miles. We sometimes played in nearby fields when our schoolyard seemed too small. Recesses were fun. We didn't have any playground equipment, but that didn't matter. We played "King on the Mountain" using dirt that bulldozers had not yet leveled.

"King on the Mountain" was a simple game. Every kid tried to surge to the top of a little hill and stay there as long as possible. Every other kid tried to push, pull, or tackle the topmost kid. I was pretty good at this game, but my coat sleeves were repeatedly ripped off my new winter jacket. My mother kindly reattached them each time.

"Please be more careful," She begged as she handed me my freshly-mended coat.

"I will," I replied but kept losing my sleeves. She kept fixing them.

We often played war games, especially snowball fights in the winter and knife fights in the summer. We used real snowballs and imaginary knives. Our rules for both games were similar. We split into two teams and attempted to "kill" each other until one team was annihilated. A kill happened when someone was struck by an enemy's "knife" or snowball. Then we were "dead" until a teammate tagged us and made us alive again.

We lived in a snow belt close to Lake Michigan, 15 miles as the crow flies, and had fresh snow all winter. This provided ample ammunition for daily battles. Although snowball fights were allowed for most of my grade school years, they were eventually abolished. My brother Bruce was responsible.

Bruce and I have different personalities, and these differences were obvious in our snowball tactics. My method involved speed and his emphasized deliberation. I scooped up snow on the run and fired rapidly. I swerved and dodged as I fired like a machine gun. I packed snowballs fast and loose, firing often and missing my target half the time. However, I fired so much that I "killed" lots of opponents.

Bruce, on the other hand, was a sniper. He lurked behind a snow fort made of huge snowballs piled atop each other. There, Bruce carefully packed each snowball, shaping and repacking until he had a perfect baseball-sized sphere. Bruce's well-packed, icy snowballs stung like crazy. Eventually, they drew enough complaints to ban all snowball fighting.

My generation enjoyed rights and freedoms that seem inconceivable to kids today. Snowball fights were the least of it. Kids today can be expelled for taking a knife to school, but we proudly carried knives everywhere. I took my first jackknife to school when I was only seven or eight years old.

Later, more kids brought knives, and we played a version of Mumblety-Peg during recess. This game involved making a mark on the ground, moving back a few feet, and throwing our knives end-over-end at the mark. The winner was the one who stuck his knife in the dirt closest to the mark.

We also loved to play marbles, and like Mumblety-Peg, it was a two-player game. We drew a circle in the dirt, put marbles in it, knelt outside, and flicked a larger marble at small ones in the middle. Winning came from knocking the other guy's marbles out before he got yours.

I also loved to wrestle at recess. No teacher ever said, "No fighting." In fact, teachers rarely appeared on the playground at all. This was their break as well as ours.

My memories of recess at South School are many, but my memories of class times are few, even though I spent nearly four years there. Art and music classes were taught by roving teachers who covered all grades in all buildings.

Once, the art teacher taught us to make papier-Mache masks. We pasted layers of paper on balloons, let them dry a week, and popped the balloons. We trimmed edges, cut holes for eyes, and started to paint them. I began with red lips, blue eyes, and brown hair but couldn't get the look I wanted. Impulsively, I smeared colors everywhere. Splotches and streaks blended together.

Suddenly, I froze. Our art teacher was silently making the rounds, inspecting each student's work. He stopped and stood over my mask. I knew I was in trouble. Then he said, "That's very nice. Very original. Good work."

My classmates crowded around and added their own compliments. I sighed in relief and accepted their praise.

Our music teacher also made rounds, which expanded in fifth grade to weekly recorder lessons. We practiced playing this simple plastic flute at home and demonstrated progress on music day. I worked diligently and dreamed of the day when I could play in a big band. My friend Alan (not the one who climbed the air shaft) wanted to play the trumpet. I shared his dream and waited expectantly for end-of-year evaluations.

Finally, the day came when our music teacher spent time with me alone. He conducted tests that measured my ability to identify distinct tones and follow rhythms. I wondered what my special talents would be. Would I be a trumpeter, a drummer, or something else?

My teacher concluded the tests and informed me, perhaps a little too bluntly, "Glen, you don't have a gift for music."

My voice trembled as I asked, "Isn't there something I could play?"

"Probably any instrument would be a waste of money for you," he said.

My heart sank. My face fell. I had been taking private piano lessons for several years, and thought I was doing well. Now I knew I was mistaken. I quickly quit playing the piano and sadly walked away from music.

Another grade school memory comes from fifth and sixth grades. My teacher was an older widow, a strong, thin woman with a fierce, deeply-lined face. She was kind but not gentle, tough as nails but deeply competent. Her name was Mrs. Shields, and she ran a farm some twenty miles away. She could and did kill rattlesnakes with a stick. She could and did put kids in their place when they needed it.

I looked up to a kid named Jay when I was a fifth-grader. He had a great sense of humor and made everyone laugh all the time. Sometimes, Mrs. Shields even cracked a smile. I wanted to be like Jay, but there was no way I could compete with his talent for comedy. I bided my time until sixth grade.

I spent the summer thinking about being funny. I was ready when school started. With Jay gone, I would be the new class comic. I sat in class and made one funny comment after another, never missing an opportunity for a punchline. Before long, Mrs. Shields stopped abruptly. She turned toward me with a rattlesnake-killing glare and said, "Glen, I don't know what's gotten into you, but I don't like it. You aren't funny, not one bit."

I swallowed hard, bit my tongue, and gave up my comedy career. Jay would reign supreme, the ever-unequalled champion.

SOUTH SCHOOL
HUDSONVILLE, MICH.
GRADES 5 & 6   1960-61

Glen's sixth grade class, with fifth grade too. Mrs. Shields is in the upper left corner. Glen is immediately to the right of "South School," etc.

Dear Grandkids,

I wish I could describe how much fun I had during my grade-school years. Both at school and at home, I had freedom to roam and play.

Your Grandma and I have tried to give you these experiences too, turning you loose when you visit. I'm glad we have fields and woods that you enjoy.

I hope you and your children inherit a world where kids are both safe and free.

Love, Grandpa Glen

Glen pulling Ross and Bruce on a sled in front of the Spring Street house.

Chapter 5 – Play Time Through the Seasons

Summers, weekends, and evenings provided ample time for play. A few kids (not me) played Little League baseball each summer. It was the only adult-run sport in town, except for high-school teams. Adults had their own lives and work. They didn't spend time hauling kids to practices.

I usually spent free time outdoors. Wintertime sledding was a frequent pastime, as we had several excellent hills just a short walk from home. I used an old wooden sled with steel runners. I kept the runners sanded and waxed for maximum speed. At the top of the sliding hill, I sprinted forward, belly-flopped onto the sled, and flew down—zig-zagging past slower sliders. I loved speed.

I also had a pair of wooden skis with simple leather straps. I would stand on the hilltop, shove off with my ski poles, and zoom straight down the hill. These skis, and my ability at skiing, gave me no control. I could go straight and fast or straight and fast. I couldn't steer but it didn't matter. I bent my knees, kept my balance, and zoomed down.

Sometimes we used our big wooden toboggan, especially when we visited our friends the Timmers. They lived a few miles away and had a huge sliding hill on one of the highest bluffs in the area. Mr. Timmer had cut a groove, about two feet deep and three feet wide, straight down the hill. It was perfect for careening downward without veering into the woods.

I went ice skating as often as possible, all winter long, keeping a section of the creek cleared of snow. It was a long narrow pool, protected by steep banks. There was no room to maneuver but it was fine for quick sprints. The town firehall, just beyond the creek, was handy as well. Firemen flooded their field each winter to make a town rink. It was big, but open to the wind and only sporadically maintained.

The best ice skating was at Porter's Pond, two miles out of town. Mr. Porter dammed a small stream in a sheltered ravine, built a little warming house, and strung electric lights. He used pumps to re-flood it nightly, and local teenagers helped to keep it clear of snow. It cost a quarter for an evening's skate.

One end of the pond usually hosted a hockey game as older boys zipped back and forth chasing the puck. The other end held a game of "Pom-pom-poll-away." One person was chosen as "it," and stood in the middle of the ice while everyone else was on the sidelines. In singles or groups, kids dashed across the ice to the other side, trying to avoid being tagged by the "it" person.

Anyone tagged also became "it." The crowd in the middle swelled as the sidelines shrank. The sidelines were "safe," but one couldn't linger long. The "it" crowd glared and chanted, "pom-pom-poll-away, come across or we'll pull you away." Then they rushed forward and pulled people into the middle. The last person tagged, zig-zagging and speeding across the pond, would be "it" for the next game. This was one of my favorite games.

One winter we had a huge and unusual storm. First, we had six or eight inches of wet, sleety snow that built up in a dense layer over bare, frozen ground. Then the sleet turned to freezing rain that saturated the top inch of dense snow. When skies cleared and temperatures dropped, the top layer froze solid. Roads were impassable. Schools were closed. My new ice rink covered the whole town and beyond. I found skiing down steep hills on skates particularly thrilling.

I loved winter, but spring also had its pleasures, especially hiking in the woods with my friend Alan. Each May first, we gathered wildflowers for May Day— Trout Lilies, Dutchman's Breeches, Violets, Blood-Root blooms, Spring Beauties, and Sweet-Williams. We arranged colorful, sweet-smelling bouquets that we took home to our mothers. The flowers stayed fresh only a day or two, but gathering them was fun.

Spring also brought schoolyard baseball games. I enjoyed playing with other kids even though I wasn't very good at the game. There were no umpires, coaches, or parents.

Spring brought a reliable run of suckers up the streams. This was before invasive sea lampreys devastated Great Lakes fishing. Dip netters with huge nets lined the edges of the Grand River, scooping up bushels of suckers to make smoked fish. Our little creek, a tributary of a tributary of the Grand, saw every deep pool filled with dozens of large fish. It was exciting trying to catch them with my little fishing pole.

Summers were delightful and almost endless. I roamed woods and fields—sometimes alone, sometimes with friends, but usually with my dog. It seemed that no place was off-limits. City yards weren't fenced and farm fields weren't posted "no trespassing." Kids could roam as far as they wanted as long as they were respectful of others' property.

My favorite walks were along the creek. Following it into the countryside, I watched for birds and butterflies. I always saw something, maybe a kingfisher darting ahead or perhaps a Great Blue Heron stalking minnows.

Following the creek into town, I lifted rocks to watch crayfish scuttle to other hiding places. Under the bridge for the four-lane highway, broad sandy beaches created a special, hidden spot. Dragonflies usually flitted near the bridge, their iridescent wings gleaming. Kids in our town were afraid of them. We called them "sewing bugs" and said, "They'll sew your eyes shut."

Sometimes I followed the creek south of town through horse pastures, farmlands, and on to a marshy area hidden in ravines and woodlands. The creek always provided endless, excellent entertainment. Even as a grade-schooler, I could be gone for hours, roaming for miles without anyone worrying.

Kids often played "Cops and Robbers," "Cowboys and Indians," or "Nazis and Americans." All of these were excuses to run around, hide behind corners, and shoot at "enemies" with toy guns on sunny afternoons. We all had toy guns, especially pistols that shot "caps." Caps were rolls of heavy red paper; two sheets glued together. The rolls were about a quarter inch wide and had thick spots, dots containing a tiny bit of explosive, spaced at regular intervals.

I loaded my gun with caps, pulled the trigger, and a puff of smoke appeared along with a loud "bang." Each pull of the trigger advanced the roll to the next cap as I shot again and again. I was a frequent customer at the corner grocery store, replenishing my caps supply.

I also had a toy pistol that shot little plastic pellets and a "pop gun," a toy rifle that made a loud noise. But I didn't play guns when my dad was around. He insisted that guns were tools, not toys. He wouldn't allow us to point a gun, even a toy one, at a person. He might not notice if I hit my brother with a stick, but I was in deep trouble if I pointed the stick and said, "bang."

My great aunt once bought me a BB gun. My dad made her return it. He didn't like something that was half toy and half weapon. Most parents were more casual about toy guns and so were the kids. A neighbor boy a block away was blind in one eye from a BB gun accident.

We kids sometimes pretended to be Indian warriors, throwing spears made of old mullein plants which had grown straight and tall on the edges of muck fields. It was great fun until one kid lost an eye when he didn't duck in time. That was the end of spear fights in our town.

Unsupervised kids can be rather reckless. I remember a "fort," a big plywood hut, that older boys made by the creek. Big "KEEP OUT" signs were painted on all sides, and the door was secured with a padlock. My friends and I once found it open and went in. There was nothing inside but old comic books. We settled down to read but soon the big kids came. As we ran away, they caught my friends but not me.

They were tossed in the creek as punishment for trespassing. I quickly climbed a tree—higher than the big kids could. One of them got close and tried to shake me loose. That didn't work, so another boy hauled up a can of muddy creek water and tossed it on me. You can't escape justice.

Autumn brought falling leaves and new kinds of fun. My parents saved maple leaves to enrich garden soil, but our leaves didn't go straight to the garden. First, we piled them below a tree and took turns jumping down. Other families burned leaf piles. We kids poked sticks at the heaps, shuffling and stirring ashes. Sometimes we roasted marshmallows or hot dogs over the fires.

Halloween soon followed. I joined packs of kids roaming town, gathering grocery bags of treats. As usual, parents were home and kids were unsupervised. Sometimes bigger boys, ones too old for trick-or-treating, demanded candy from youngsters. It was the price we paid for a world where adults were absent. Bullying happened. We had to deal with it the best we could.

Dear Grandkids,

My parents were peculiar, especially my dad. He was extremely generous and loved the natural world. He also loved The Bible and church. I hope some of this has been passed down to me and on to you.

However, my dad had little empathy and deeply lacked an ability to see another person's point of view. He loved talking but was a poor listener.

I hope I've learned to be the person I am both by his example of what to be and his example of what not to be.

I hope that you, too, can learn from my example, whether good or bad.

Love, Grandpa Glen

The air raid on Bari in 1943.

Chapter 6—My Parents

Stan spent World War II in the Navy on the USS *Aroostook*, a tanker with the dangerous task of transporting gasoline to remote stations around the Mediterranean Sea. The *Aroostook*, newly loaded with fresh fuel, was tied up at Bari, Italy, on December 2, 1943. German planes came in a surprise raid that night.

The port of Bari was brightly lit to permit round-the-clock loading and unloading. It had almost no air defenses, neither guns nor fighter planes. The harbor was full of tightly packed ships—sitting ducks for any attack—but the port's Allied Commander, British Air Marshal Sir Arthur Coningham, was unconcerned. He held a press conference that afternoon and assured everyone that the port was perfectly safe. He explained that Germany's Luftwaffe was too battered to be dangerous.

That night, one hundred and five German bombers achieved complete surprise. They bombed the brightly-lit harbor with great accuracy. Ammunition ship explosions shattered windows seven miles away. When a dockside pipeline burst, gushing gasoline spread a sheet of flame across the harbor. This attack saw dozens of ships and thousands of lives lost—Pearl Harbor all over again.

One wrecked ship released mustard gas across the harbor and city. Mustard gas was banned after World War I, but Americans had a secret shipload in case Germans used it first. The shipment was still top-secret so none of the thousands of victims were properly diagnosed or treated after exposure.

Meanwhile, Stan was on a ship full of fuel while one hundred and five German bombers screamed overhead. My father was a man of deep principles and fervent Christian convictions. He could also be ungracious and abrasive. He never drank alcohol, never played cards, never flirted with women, and never smoked cigarettes. He invited teasing, even bullying, over his convictions and behavior.

However, on the night of December 2, 1943, two of his former tormentors sat in his lap for a long and hellish time. They figured Stan might have some "in" with The Almighty. They wanted to be close, just in case. Indeed, their ship and all its men were spared.

I think my dad suffered what would later be called Post Traumatic Stress Disorder. However, his defining characteristic was determination, not disorder. He did not let circumstances or experiences stop him from doing what needed to be done. His determination mattered when that deadly tornado hit Hudsonville in the spring of 1956. My father spent that night as a volunteer searching for casualties. He felt his war-time trauma had prepared him for this grim task.

Our family always enjoyed Hudsonville's Fourth of July fireworks. Every year my dad would claim he was tired and go back to the car. Decades later we learned that he spent each fireworks evening lying in the back seat with his eyes shut and ears covered. He let us enjoy the flash and boom, but it was too much like an air raid for him.

My father was deeply affected by wartime experiences, but other traits were his since birth. He tended to be intensely dedicated to an interest or activity, or he would forget it completely and move on. He was very sensitive to his own feelings but quite oblivious to other people's moods or emotions. He was an avid talker but a poor listener. He may have had high-functioning Asperger Syndrome. Wikipedia describes it as, "A developmental disorder characterized by significant difficulties in social interaction and nonverbal communication, along with restricted and repetitive patterns of behavior and interests."

He was easily frustrated and prone to losing his temper in an instant, at least with us kids. He spanked us with his belt when we misbehaved. He disciplined impulsively without checking to see what happened or why. One kid and another would be spanked as the story slowly emerged, often after the innocent had already been punished with the guilty.

I was just as determined as my father and took spankings without a whimper. Ross was smarter and cried loud and hard until the spanking stopped. This usually made his spankings lighter and shorter, but he once mistimed it and cried before being hit. That didn't help!

My dad never hit my mother but would sometimes yell and throw things. We had a big desk in the living room that tended to collect magazines, newspapers, and old mail. When the desk got bad and my dad couldn't find something, he would sweep the whole mess to the floor. Then he would yell at my mother, make her pick it up, and insist she find what he wanted. She always complied, sobbing great tears as she sorted the pile.

Ellen was the fixer; she could talk my dad down from his rage and make him feel ashamed of his bad behavior. Then he became extremely apologetic and tried to make it up with sweetness and humility.

I think that much of my dad's anger came from his stress at work. He was deeply committed to his job as an Electrical Engineer. He worked long hours each weekday and often half of Saturday as well. His work kept him wound up. Even on vacation, he didn't completely relax for several days. Then he was pleasant and fun for the rest of our time.

Whenever and wherever we camped, he made daily phone calls to troubleshoot problems at the office. Long-distance calls were expensive, so my dad placed "collect" calls from pay phones, asking "Mr. Stanley" to accept the charges. Calls were accepted when something needed attention but otherwise declined.

My dad was good at his work, perhaps even brilliant. His company made manufacturing equipment that "Big Three" automakers used to make cars. He often went to Detroit to troubleshoot equipment in place. He received many job offers but declined them all. He wanted to raise his family in Hudsonville, not Detroit. A Ford executive once asked him, "How much will it take for you to accept a job here."

"Ford doesn't have that much money," was his answer.

My dad also served as chairman of the board for many church, community, and professional organizations. He was often away at meetings after long days at work. All this meant that his home time was his rest time, and he didn't do much around the house.

My mother wasn't much of a housekeeper either. She was smart and capable at many things, but housekeeping was outside her field of interest. My siblings and I did some of the cooking, all the dishwashing, and most other cleaning. Our chores included summertime lawn and garden work as well as wintertime snow removal.

Scrubbing the kitchen floor was one of our harder chores. The old, cream-colored tiles were pitted and worn. Dirt worked its way into their surfaces and didn't come out easily. I discovered that the best way to clean the floor was to saturate it with soapy water. Then I let it sit a while before scrubbing it. This led to an inventive cleaning technique.

Sometimes, when both my parents and Ellen were gone for an evening, I was in charge of chores and siblings. I took the opportunity to instigate water fights in the kitchen after dishes were done. Then we mopped up, especially the floor, before our parents came home. They always praised us for a job well done.

This practice ceased when my parents returned early once. As usual, there was no time for explanation. My dad grabbed squirt guns and stomped them to bits. Marian protested that she hadn't taken part in the water fight, but her squirt gun was already smashed. My dad gave her Ross's gun, the best one of all. That was the end of a pleasant way to do an unpleasant chore.

My Aunt once saw her kids, my older cousins, playing a make-believe game of "Margaret and Stanley." Darlene was Margaret; Dale was Stanley.

"Hurry up, we're late for church," said "Stanley."

"Stanley, look at all these kids," replied "Margaret," "You can at least help!"

Darlene nailed it, but the real Margaret and Stanley never changed their dynamics. Because my father was gone a lot, our homelife was shaped more by my mother's patience than my father's lack of it.

I remember one time when I pushed my mother too far. Over at the schoolyard, I catapulted rocks off a slide until one flew wrong and struck my forehead. I ran home with blood streaming down my face, stopped outside the door, and called in a cheery voice, "Momma, come see." She popped out and screamed in terror, terror that turned to anger when she saw it was only a superficial wound.

She was so tolerant that my brothers and I, as young teens, target-practiced with a 22-caliber rifle in the basement, firing into a backstop. Meanwhile, she sat upstairs reading.

Dear Grandkids,

I loved climbing trees when I was a boy. Tree climbing was a skill that I taught myself through constant practice, climbing all kinds of trees in all kinds of conditions.

I learned which branches were strong and which were weak, and I learned how this varied from an oak to a maple to a willow.

I know that most of you like tree climbing also. Isn't it fun to be on top of the world?

Love Grandpa Glen

Glen on his bike
in back
of the Spring Street
house.

Chapter 7—Playing and Working

I taught myself to climb across our yard on big maple trees, going from branch to branch and tree to tree without touching the ground. I was always aware of possible danger. I learned to time handholds and footholds so I didn't depend on just one hold at a time. I also planned, with every move, where I would catch myself if I fell.

My tree climbing included watching for bird nests each spring. I once found a red-tailed-hawk nest eighty feet up a beech tree. I climbed above it and peered down from an overhanging branch. It held several eggs. I kept coming back for several weeks as the eggs became naked hatchlings, then fledglings, and finally full-sized hawks. The full-sized hawks, still in the nest, had fierce eyes and talons like molten gold.

This was interesting but not wise. I kept expecting adult hawks to swoop at me while I was eighty feet off the ground, though it never happened. Hawks were far less common then. Farmers killed them since they sometimes preyed on chickens. Perhaps they did, but I only saw dead rats at the nest.

I loved running and walking with my dog, Shadow, as my companion. We wandered far and wide, for hours at a time. Shadow was a mongrel, a mutt. Maybe his bloodline held hunting dogs somewhere; he looked like an Irish Setter—a small, black one.

Shadow had a great personality. He was active, affectionate and gentle. One time, he nosed into some fishing poles and got a hook in his lip. We ran for wire cutters, snipped the barb, and pulled the hook out. He stood still through the whole operation, never whining or growling.

Shadow was normally on a chain, but occasionally we let him run free. He would rocket away and be gone for hours. When our city enacted a leash law that prohibited free-ranging dogs, we were obligated to obey it. Shadow grew impatient with his confinement on a short fifteen-foot chain.

When I was young there were many pheasants in the fields around Hudsonville. Fall pheasant hunting was a popular sport. My friends and I (sometimes with Shadow along) roamed fields collecting spent shotgun shells. We made a game of seeing who could find the most.

Later, we begged tail feathers from successful hunters. We stuck several long feathers in an empty shotgun shell and crimped it shut. These pheasant feather/shotgun shell darts (without points) had excellent balance and flew straight and true. We had pheasant-feather-dart wars (like snowball fights) or threw at trees to see who had the best aim.

Sometimes, I went along with my dad when he went hunting. We brought Shadow too. My dad's expectations of the dog seemed unreasonably high. He wanted him to behave like a well-trained bird dog, but Shadow had no training at all. He didn't know simple commands like "sit" or "stay," let alone the finer points of hunting. He didn't even know he was hunting.

On a hunting trip, Shadow loved the freedom of being off the chain. He raced through fields and woods. He stopped to sniff hunters and other dogs. Sometimes he accidently flushed a bird within shooting range, but not often. My father grew frustrated and angry, expecting Shadow to be something he wasn't, and expecting me to make it so.

I loved riding my bike almost as much as I loved running and climbing. I could ride as far as I wanted. Sometimes I rode five miles to a friend's home in the next town. We shot his bow and arrow, threw stones at pigeons in the barn, and explored a nearby woods. Once we discovered a little cave, a great wonder in our rock-less area.

I liked swimming, but since Hudsonville had nowhere to swim, my parents often drove us to parks fifteen or twenty miles away. My dad didn't swim much. His time in the Mediterranean had ruined him for anything less than warm water. We especially enjoyed Lake Michigan parks with their dunes, waves, and driftwood. My dad never cooked at home but always grilled excellent burgers and hot dogs on a picnic.

My boyhood wasn't all playtime. I also worked, especially during onion harvest. Onions grew in long rows in vast muck fields. Kids worked side by side with other kids in other rows. We pulled onions, snipped tops, and tossed them aside. Topless onions fell into a crate which we dragged along until full. Fast, persistent kids filled one hundred crates a day and earned ten dollars. That translates to eighty-five dollars a day and a thousand dollars a season in 2020 dollars.

Other workers, Mexican migrants, worked far in the distance—men, women, and children together. We never worked side by side or talked to each other. I never knew where they lived or what they ate. They were off in the distance, just a part of the landscape.

At other times during the summer I might pick strawberries, peaches or apples. I rode my bike each harvest day, traveling up to eight miles one way. I liked picking blueberries best. It didn't pay as well as some crops, but its season was longer and I never tired of eating as I picked.

I grew up in a time and place where a kid could earn lots of money and have lots of fun.

Glen still enjoys playing but now it's with grandkids.

Dear Grandkids,

My family took many camping trips when I was young.

No other kids in town traveled like we did. People used to think we were poor, but suddenly we seemed rich.

We took our first long trip during the summer before I turned ten. My dad had a special opportunity and decided to make the most of it.

This was the vacation that got us started on a series of camping trips.

I'm going to tell how it all started.

      Love, Grandpa Glen

The Van Antwerp family camping
by a lake in the Rocky Mountains.
Note the tent and cartop carrier.

Chapter 8 – First Camping Trip

My dad became President of the West Michigan Chapter of the American Institute of Electrical Engineers in the late 1950s. This organization later merged with IRE to become the IEEE. The Institute's national convention was slated for Seattle, Washington, in the summer of 1959. My father could go for free. As chapter president, all his airfare, food, and lodging would be covered.

He calculated and negotiated an arrangement that paid him a lump sum instead of expenses. He could spend it as he chose. He opted to travel cheap and scheduled his annual vacation to bracket the conference dates. Now he had the time and means to take our whole family along. He made these arrangements without telling us kids. Then he asked, "If you could travel anywhere in the United States where would you go?"

Ellen picked, "Niagara Falls!"

I had never seen mountains but already loved them. I voted, "Yellowstone!"

The younger kids had no opinion. Ellen and I argued our cases while my dad quietly grinned. I pulled an encyclopedia to show that Yellowstone's falls were taller than Niagara's.

"Besides," I added, "Yellowstone has mountains, geysers, bears, buffalo, elk, moose, and more!"

Ellen was eager to please, as always. "Yellowstone would be alright," she agreed.

"We'll go to Yellowstone," my father smiled and said, "we'll go to Yellowstone and beyond."

He laid out an itinerary and helped us write to towns and parks along the way. Our excitement grew as daily mail brought brochures about places we'd visit.

Preparations began. My dad designed a car top carrier. It had to be big to match our family size. It would be aerodynamic to give good gas mileage, and would be sturdy but lightweight. Finally, he had what he wanted—a wide, long, aluminum box with rounded ends. The water-tight cover would come off for easy access. This cover would have fittings for attachable legs in case we needed a spare picnic table.

My dad took his design to a sheet metal shop to have the carrier completed. It was big—thirty cubic feet of storage—and shiny. It looked odd atop our four-door family sedan. But it worked incredibly well.

We bought a tent that would hold the whole family, made of heavy canvas and shaped like a small house. Each sidewall was four feet high, and the roof rose to a six-foot center. It was nine feet wide and twelve feet long, just the right size for seven sleeping bags and a few suitcases.

Next, we acquired sleeping bags, all of them used— some borrowed, some purchased. We bought and packed other supplies.

The final Friday came. Our adventure began when my dad came home from work a little early. The car and carrier were already loaded. We stuffed last-minute items in the crowded trunk, squeezed into our seats, and zoomed off.

We drove north to Big Rapids and left my little sister, Marian, with Uncle Alan and Aunt Leah. They would care for her while we were gone for two weeks. My parents figured that a long road trip would be too much for her since she was not yet two. She was cute and precocious, and we would miss her terribly.

The car-ferry took us from Ludington, Michigan, to Manitowoc, Wisconsin. We drove west daily, entranced by the scenery. Our familiar landscapes of fields and woodlots gradually gave way to vast prairies. The route, mostly US-2, took us through several cities and many small towns.

We entertained ourselves with endless rounds of the alphabet game (checking roadside signs for an "A," a "B," etc.) We also kept a list of license plates to see how many states we could find.

I was surprised to see that the Great Plains were not necessarily flat. Sometimes they spread to the horizon in long, gentle swells. The wheat and corn fields, which had dominated the landscape, started to include stretches of grazing land. Then we traveled through grasslands with few crops or homes. The deer and the antelope played. Cattle too. The horizon stretched on forever.

We camped each evening and soon became adept at setting up. My dad cranked his car window all the way open. He hopped up and stood there, handing carrier items down. First came the plastic ground cloth, then tent and poles, next sleeping bags and suitcases.

We boys cleared sticks and stones from a tent spot, laid out the ground cloth, and erected the tent. Our sleeping bags were always laid out in the same order. My parents, in their double bag, were next to the door with the other kids beside them. I had my bag at their feet. Any remaining space served as an entry way and a place for suitcases and shoes.

My mother took the food, stove, and picnic supplies out of the trunk to start supper. Sometimes we pulled in late and did all this by the car's headlights.

As we traveled the rolling prairies on US-2, the mountains of Glacier National Park grew larger and nearer. Finally, we passed lovely Saint Mary Lake and began climbing the "Going to the Sun" highway.

Every pass and switchback showed amazing vistas as we climbed higher and higher. Steep cliffs and countless waterfalls rose on the mountain side. Low stone walls guarding precipitous drop-offs were on the other side. Majestic glaciers and stunning mountain peaks surrounded us. It was even better than I expected.

After Glacier National Park, we continued west across Idaho into Washington. We traveled vast rolling wheat lands before descending to the Columbia River with its beautiful orchard country. Then we climbed mountains again through the rugged Cascades before descending to the sea and Seattle. It held half a million people, the largest city in the whole Northwest.

We stayed at a nice campground out of town. Each morning my dad got ready and went to his conference. He shaved and showered at camp, donned a suit and tie, and drove us to the city. We went sight-seeing. He attended meetings. Each evening we all went back to camp. There, he changed clothes and we had our usual picnic supper.

After the conference we explored Olympia National Park. We loved its stunning mountains and magnificent rainforests. We were fascinated by its beaches—so different from Lake Michigan shorelines. At low tide we watched people digging for clams. Crystal-clear tidal pools filled with starfish, sea anemones, and other exotic creatures enchanted us.

After touring Washington, we dropped down to Oregon and entered Idaho. The weird lava lands of Craters of the Moon National Monument were exotic indeed. Then we came to Yellowstone National Park. It was everything I hoped for and more. The geysers, falls, and wildlife were fantastic. We fished on Yellowstone Lake and had a nice trout supper.

Bears roamed roadsides and campgrounds, looking for leftovers or handouts. We never had food in the tent, nor did we leave any lying about. We preferred to see our bears and other wildlife at a decent distance.

We proceeded east after Yellowstone and motored over Powder River Pass after dark. We searched for a campground but couldn't find one. This was open-range country with black Angus steers roaming the black highway in the black of night, but fortunately, we avoided a cow-car accident.

When a campground sign appeared, we turned down a rutted, stony track. A boulder caught our muffler and tore it off. We roared into the campground, waking the few campers who were already there.

Despite the introduction, I fell in love with Crazy Woman Creek National Forest Campground. Our tent sat fifteen feet from a bubbling rapids that sang all night. We woke in the morning to a bright blue sky, overhead pines, foaming cascades, and glorious mountain peaks. I still love this campground and have been back several times.

We got our muffler replaced in Buffalo, Wyoming. Then it was on to South Dakota and the Black Hills. There, we toured Wind and Jewell caves, saw Mount Rushmore, and drove through Custer State Park. Herds of buffalo roamed free. We toured the Badlands with their vivid colors and strangely eroded landscapes.

After a quick stop at Wall Drug (see the stuffed jackalopes!), we again crossed Minnesota and Wisconsin before coming to Michigan's Upper Peninsula. We crossed the new Mackinaw Bridge for our first time ever, crowding windows for a better view of the tiny boats below.

We made one final stop, to pick up Marian in Big Rapids, and proceeded home. We had traveled thousands of miles in 16 days. This trip set a pattern for later ones. We rarely stayed two nights in any given place and usually drove hundreds of miles almost every day. It wasn't particularly restful, but we saw lots of country.

Dear Grandkids,

I loved visiting grandparents up north, in Osceola County, Michigan.

It was a three-hour trip on busy two-lane roads. Expressways didn't exist on our side of the state yet.

My house, today, is on the farm where my Van Antwerp grandparents lived when I was young. In a way, you repeat my childhood visits any time you come to see Grandma and me.

I make maple syrup each spring on the farm where my Dahlstrom grandparents lived. You've been there too.

Your Grandma and I enjoy your visits just as much as I enjoyed visiting my grandparents.

Love, Grandpa Glen

Uncle George Bennard at home on the Dahlstrom farm.

Glen still uses the Dahlstrom sugar house to make maple syrup.

Chapter 9 – Grandparents

Trips to visit grandparents were always adventures. The highway was hilly and busy. Double yellow lines marked the many no-passing zones. My dad drove fast, waiting impatiently for breaks in traffic. In those days, before freeways and cruise control, my dad's driving was: stomp on gas, slam on brakes, veer in, swerve out, gain a car length. Some kid usually got sick. We always had a puke can along just in case.

My two sets of grandparents were different in many ways. Grandpa Dahlstrom was the first in his neighborhood to buy a car. He wired his house for electricity before electric lines came through. Grandpa Van (Antwerp) was more conservative. He had an outhouse—no indoor plumbing. Woodstoves—no central heating. Grandpa Van subsistence farmed with horse-drawn equipment. Grandpa Dahlstrom earned a respectable income as an independent house painter.

Cousins lived close to my grandparents at both places, so I always had playmates. When we visited Grandma Dahlstrom's, I usually explored a nearby creek and beaver pond. One time, I found a large brown trout just below the dam. I caught it by hand, but it slipped back and rocketed away.

Aunt Hannah and Uncle George, Grandpa Dahlstrom's sister and her husband, lived next door. We adored them and they doted on us. Uncle George was famous—the composer of "The Old Rugged Cross." He was in his 80s with flowing, snow-white hair. He looked old but his mind was sharp and witty.

My dad once bragged, "I've had a car all these years and never had a wreck."

Uncle George glanced at our automobile, the current clunker in a string of very-used cars. "No, Stanley,'" he slyly said, "you've had a wreck all these years and never had a car."

On another occasion, Aunt Hannah was trying to learn to drive. A middle-aged Methodist preacher lady served as Hannah's rather unsuccessful instructor. Aunt Hannah had drifted off the driveway into soft sand. The more she spun her wheels, the worse it got. My dad was pushing and yelling, "Rock it, rock it!"

This was the time when singers like Elvis Presley, Chuck Berry, and Buddy Holly were pioneering "Rock and Roll." Uncle George, an eighty-five-year-old hymn writer, stood by in mild amusement and cracked, "She's rocking it Stanley, but it won't roll."

My mother's youngest brother shared my dad's name. Uncle Stanley's age was halfway between mine and my mom's. He was still in college when I was in grade school. Sometimes he was home and still asleep when we got to Grandma's house. We kids ran upstairs, burst through his doorway, and pounced on his bed. He pretended to sleep, "snoring" ever more loudly. Then he suddenly roared and chased us downstairs. We loved that game.

Uncle Stanley always loved to have fun. One winter day, he took my brothers and me to a shallow pond in a nearby field and asked, "Did you ever play rubber ice?"

"No, what's that?"

"Rubber ice is a game for a day like this," Uncle Stanley explained.

"Why, what's special today?"

"Several things," he replied. "This pond just froze in last-night's cold snap. The ice is thin, strong, and free of snow."

Then Stanley shouted, "Watch me," as he shuffled quickly across the pond, never raising his feet. The ice stayed solid. "You're next," he called to me.

I zipped across, going straight and fast without lifting my feet. Bruce and Ross followed. We kept taking turns as the once-solid ice developed a maze of hairline cracks. The cracks grew and the ice began to buckle and wave under us. Now we saw "rubber ice" for ourselves.

My brother sped across. His feet left tiny pools across the broken ice. My turn. I took a deep breath and zipped smoothly along. The ice rose and fell by six or eight inches with every slide, but it still held me up. Then it didn't. The ice gave way and I was drenched in freezing water. Everybody laughed as we hurried back to Grandma's for a change of clothes.

Grandma Dahlstrom was a good cook. Her fare was always plentiful, varied, and delicious. She was so good that she earned extra cash running a home "restaurant" during the depression. She advertised "home-cooked country dinners" and took reservations. On appointed evenings, several well-to-do city couples came for dinner. The rest of the family made themselves scarce as Grandma served her tasty dishes and collected her pay.

We ate meals at Grandma Dahlstrom's more than at Grandma Van's. This was partly due to our usual schedule, and partly because Grandma Van offered less variety. Her food was well-prepared but followed a very Scottish pattern of simplicity and efficiency. For instance, breakfast was always oatmeal and pancakes. It was good oatmeal and good pancakes, but never anything else.

I didn't mind sameness when it came to Grandma Van's bread, baked in the wood stove, and served with homemade butter. It was always delicious.

The Van Antwerp farm was a mile long. The south side held the house and barn. The other end was all woods. Hayfields occupied the middle. My dad once drove me to the north end on an early-June day. "Walk back to the house," he said, "It will be fun."

"I might get lost."

"You won't. The road is on your east, the line fence is west—don't cross them. Keep going south, toward the noonday sun."

I walked quietly, watching birds flitting in the trees and listening to their songs. A partridge waited unseen until I was close. Then it flew off like a noisy rocket and scared me half to death. I paused, caught my breath, and moved on. Suddenly, I stopped in surprise. A small, spotted fawn lay so still that I almost stepped on it. Its big brown eyes stared at me and I stared back.

I carefully backed away as it lay motionless. I walked on, no longer nervous, but filled with excitement. Coming out of the woods, I ran across the hay fields and burst through the farmhouse door. "Hey, everybody," I called, "Guess what I saw!"

Grandpa Van's barn was a favorite play place for all the cousins. We petted cows and horses in their stalls and climbed a ladder to the hayloft piled high with loose hay. My cousins and I had free rein to run, jump, slide, and tunnel in the hay. Sometimes we pitched it down to the center of the ground floor, making a big haystack, and took turns jumping into it.

This fun lasted until one Christmas when my cousin, Virginia, slipped and cut her arm on a jagged board. It opened a huge gash that required an emergency room visit and many stitches. That was the end of unsupervised play in the barn.

I especially liked going north during maple syrup season each spring. Grandpa Dahlstrom's "sugar bush" was a grove of five hundred mature trees on the back end of his farm. His sugar house sat in the middle. Each maple tree was "tapped" with at least one tap. That is, Grandpa would drill a hole, drive a little funnel or "spile" into the hole, and hang a bucket on the spile. Each bucket collected a steady drip, drip, drip of sweet sap on warm days, days that alternated with freezing nights.

We ran from tree to tree, emptying buckets into large gathering tanks that we took back to the sugar house. Short cement walls, three feet apart, stretched from a chimney at the far end of the sugar house and reached almost to the front door. Big steel pans spanned the distance between them, making a firebox beneath. These pans, filled with sap, sent sweet steam swirling up and out an opening in the roof.

Grandpa kept the fire roaring and made sure the boiling pans were full of ever-thickening sap. He watched carefully and pulled it from the fire just as it reached syrup stage. He filled ten-gallon "cream cans" and hauled them to the house for final processing. Grandpa Dahlstrom had a good-sized operation and earned extra money selling syrup.

Grandpa Van's syrup production was much smaller. He made enough for family use. No sales. But Grandma Van made sugaring especially fun for us grandkids. She took some syrup and cooked it slowly and carefully. It grew thicker and thicker. Then she pulled the pan from the stove and got ice cubes from the freezer. We each poured a tiny puddle of hot syrup onto an ice cube. Then we pealed the taffy-like candy off the ice and devoured a delicious treat.

Grandma wasn't done yet. She put the thick syrup back on the stove and stirred carefully. The syrup gradually turned a light-brown color as it began to crystalize. She quickly poured it onto cookie sheets where it cooled to become maple sugar. We always took a batch home. I loved sugar season.

Dear Grandkids,

When I was a kid, elementary school included kindergarten through sixth grade. Junior-high was seventh and eighth grades, while high school held ninth through twelfth.

I liked grade school and high school, but junior high was hard. Maybe it is for everybody.

I hope that you do well in all your grades.

Love, Grandpa Glen

Glen and Aleta, Seventh-Grade honor guards for Eighth-Grade graduation.

Chapter 10 - Junior High School

As I approached seventh grade, Hudsonville schools—except for the new elementary buildings—were again overcrowded. All junior high students would move to elementary school classrooms to make room at the High School. One South School seventh-grader needed to go to Park to balance class sizes. I was the one.

My introduction to Park School felt awkward and uncomfortable. Many classmates were new kids from other districts. Even kids I'd known years earlier were now unfamiliar. I also felt awkward for another reason. I had a fall birthday and was the smallest and youngest student.

I was so small that my brother Bruce, two years younger, was bigger. I turned twelve years old that October and received both a shotgun and a hunting license for my birthday. My license listed my height as four feet, ten inches tall, with a weight of seventy-two pounds.

My father, who would not let me have a BB-gun when I was younger, felt that a 12-year-old was old enough, and responsible enough, for a 20-gauge shotgun. It was a tool, not a toy. Twelve was the minimum age for hunting small game. I was small but the game was smaller. I could carry a gun.

My dad grew up on a farm. He hunted often and became an excellent hunter and competent marksman. He told me about one lesson he learned as a teenager. He was walking close to a pond and saw two ducks take off. He aimed at the first but shot the second. From then on, whenever he shot a flying bird, he always aimed at an imaginary one—just the right distance ahead of the real one. I heard the story and understood the concept but could never master it.

Weekend days, whether hunting or not, were times I enjoyed. School days were difficult. I was usually teased at lunchtime by eighth-graders from another classroom. Their teasing wasn't very mean, they may have meant it in a goodhearted way, but it was constant. One of them once asked, "Why are your lips dark; do you wear lipstick?"

"I guess I'm healthy," I blurted as I grasped for a clever reply.

They laughed and nicknamed me, "Healthy Kid."

I guess I was strong and healthy for my size. President Kennedy was our new president. His concern for physical fitness started trickling down to schools—even Hudsonville ones. Students did exercises and teachers recorded results. I found that I could outdo classmates in almost all categories.

Meanwhile, drillers discovered oil on Grandpa Van's farm. My grandparents didn't get rich but were able to change some things. My grandfather retired—he was seventy-six years old and never loved farming. He sold the cows and horses. They updated the farmhouse, adding an enclosed front porch, a roomy kitchen, a whole-house furnace, and an indoor bathroom.

Now grandpa could do the things he liked. On one weekend visit, I saw him whittling by the kitchen stove.

His chips fell into the wood box. He stopped when I asked, "What are you making?"

"I'm carving a cedar fan from a single piece of wood," he said. "It's something I learned as a young lumberjack."

I was fascinated. When it was time to leave, he gave me some suitable cedar. At home, with my dad's help, I made my first fan. I proudly took it to school to show off. My teacher was impressed and offered to buy one if I made another. I happily carved one, sold it, and have been hooked on fan carving ever since. Here was a talent uniquely my own.

I felt isolated and out of place at Park School. I told my dad, and we arranged a meeting with the principal. I explained my situation and got permission to switch back to South. I had no idea what awaited me.

When I went back, my old grade-school friends were a minority and new kids ruled the roost. One of them especially disliked me. He thought I needed to know who was boss. Every day he cornered me on the playground and gathered his friends. He wrestled me to the ground, sat on me, and rapped his knuckles on my chest.

"Van Antwerp," he taunted daily, "I'm going to keep this up until you cry."

I could have been smart. I could have called it quits and cried. Instead, I was proud and defiant. I laughed in his face and mocked him. I said, "You're a baby who can't pick on somebody your own size. I'm twice the man you are."

Eventually, in my proud and defiant way, I won. His friends tired of the game and called him off. I never cried but I lost my taste for wrestling and fighting. I no longer wanted to be king on the mountain. I just wanted to be left alone.

I picked up the biggest book in the school library, *The Count of Monte Christo* by Alexander Dumas, and stayed inside to read at lunch times. By then, it was spring and most of the kids played baseball at recess. Even our teacher joined the game and urged me to come outside to play, but I stayed in with my book. Like my mother, I learned to disappear into the world of literature.

As the school year ended, two seventh-grade students were chosen as "Honor Guards" for eighth-grade graduation. A girl named Aleta and myself were picked. She towered over me as we marched into the ceremony. She must have been five feet, four inches tall.

The next school year brought all eighth-graders in the district to a couple classrooms at Park School. My sister Marian's kindergarten was also there. I walked her back and forth a few times to show her the way. Then she was on her own because our school days had different start times. She was still a few weeks shy of her fifth birthday but walked the whole way (over a mile) twice a day, on her own. Nobody thought anything of it.

I don't remember much of my eighth-grade school year except that I was usually late, or barely on time, every day. I ran most of the way to school and would charge in the door just as the final bell rang.

I also remember that I was tired of being teased for being a smart kid who knew all the answers. Then I went through a period of ignoring lessons and getting Cs and Ds instead of As. My junior-high school years were not my best years.

Glen's 8th grade school picture.

Dear Grandkids,

After our first camping trip in 1959, we continued taking vacations each summer. We alternated between east and west, north and south, adding new states and new sites each year.

My dad appreciated the educational aspect of our trips. He said, "I used to think we couldn't afford to travel. Now I think we can't afford not to."

I distinctly remember one experience on a Sunday morning in Arkansas when our white, northern family was warmly welcomed by an African-American congregation. This was one example from hundreds of times when we experienced hospitality from strangers.

After a few years we had visited every one of the forty-eight contiguous states.

Let me tell you about a couple of those trips.

Love, Grandpa Glen

Marian sitting on four states at once where Colorado, New Mexico, Arizona, and Utah meet. We had the early-morning spot to ourselves.

Chapter 11 – More Trips

One trip west took us longer and farther than previous vacations. Leaving on a Thursday, instead of our usual Friday, we headed to Kansas and visited Dahlstrom cousins there. I remember a pleasant evening capturing fireflies in their yard. The next day we drove across Kansas, Oklahoma, Texas, and northern New Mexico. We covered 1,500 miles in our first two-and-a-half days. These distances don't seem impressive now, but they were exceptional in those times before expressways.

We piled in on Van Antwerp cousins that Saturday evening. Uncle Alan, a professor at Ferris State University, was temporarily a student in Las Vegas, New Mexico—via a National Science Foundation grant. The name "Las Vegas" means "The Meadows." Both Nevada and Arizona have towns so named for grasslands that once surrounded them. Las Vegas, New Mexico, had a long Spanish history and was still a very Mexican city. We went to church with Uncle Alan, Aunt Leah, and our cousins on Sunday morning. We were happy that the pastor added English comments to his Spanish sermon.

We drove 200 miles that afternoon and camped near the Arizona border. Then we drove to Nogales, Mexico, and enjoyed its open-air market. We pressed on to central Sonora for an outstanding meal. The exchange rate must have been great. Our frugal family hardly ever ate in a restaurant, but here we enjoyed an exotic feast, served by impeccable waiters in a palatial dining hall.

We turned north and camped that night in Organ Pipe Cactus National Monument, back in the USA. We made camp by headlights as a pack of coyotes echoed their eerie calls through the hills.

Next, our trip took us to the Grand Canyon, quite a sight for a kid from the flat fields of Hudsonville. We cut across Utah and Nevada, made our way over California's Mojave Desert, and camped by the Pacific Ocean north of Los Angeles. From there we cruised California's Central Valley and went to the magnificent Sequoia, Kings Canyon, and Yosemite National Parks. We enjoyed beautiful weather every day.

In Yosemite, we met a man with a motorhome—the first one we'd ever seen. He had created it himself on an old truck chassis. I always wondered if that lone California tinkerer started the whole RV craze.

From California, we scooted up past the Great Salt Lake in Utah and were amazed at the abundance of waterfowl along its shores. We went up to Yellowstone, spent a few days, and proceeded through Wyoming's majestic Big Horn Mountains and South Dakota's scenic Black Hills.

We continued crossing South Dakota, Minnesota, Wisconsin, Illinois, and Indiana—arriving home with 24 days and 8,000 miles behind us. I was a traveler no more—just another Hudsonville kid topping onions.

Another summer trip took us northeast. This would be Ellen's last trip with the family, as she had graduated from high school and would soon start nurses' training. That first afternoon we drove 250 miles and camped east of Toledo beside Lake Erie. The next day we drove 550 miles across Ohio, Pennsylvania and New Jersey before staying in a motel near New York City. This was my first hotel experience, and our next night was even more exotic when we stayed at a hotel in New York City itself.

We spent two full days in the city. One day we visited the Statue of Liberty and the Empire State Building, where I threw paper airplanes from the top and watched them sail over the streets and buildings below. We spent our other day at the New York World's Fair, the biggest world's fair ever held in the United States.

World's Fair tickets were a dollar apiece for kids and two dollars for teenagers or adults. This totaled $11 for our family, or about ninety dollars at 2020 rates. Our city stay even had us eating in restaurants, spending money at every turn.

The fair showcased an automated, life-sized statue of President Abraham Lincoln. It was a wonder for its time with thousands of lifelike movements. He rose from his chair and recited portions of his best-known speeches, including the Gettysburg Address.

Another special exhibit, a boat ride "around the world," cost a dollar for adults and sixty cents for children. Automated children in their native costumes sang "It's a Small World After All," and the catchy tune stuck in my head for days.

On our way out of the city, we passed the New York Yankee's baseball stadium. They were playing the Detroit Tigers that day. My brother, Bruce, was a big Tigers fan and wanted to stop. My dad, not a sports fan himself, graciously tossed our schedule aside and took the younger kids in for the rest of the game while Ellen, my mother, and I waited in the car.

That evening we drove several miles to spend the night with my mother's cousin in Mamaroneck, a northern suburb of New York City. From there we traveled to the northeastern corner of Connecticut and camped two nights at Mashamoquet Brook State Park, making daytime trips through Rhode Island and Massachusetts. We toured many historic sites in and around Boston, including Revolutionary War battlefields at Lexington and Concord. I especially enjoyed the outdoor living-history museum at Old Sturbridge Village.

Next, we went through Vermont and spent a couple of nights in the White Mountains of New Hampshire. I loved the rugged mountains, the austere beauty of The Flume Gorge, and the iconic Old Man of the Mountains outcropping.

Then we headed up the coast of Maine and came to Acadia National Park. Our family, a family that could tour Boston in an afternoon and New York City in a day or two, spent three days exploring Acadia. We hiked through the woods on Mount Desert and explored tidal pools along the rocky coastline.

We continued north through Maine, cut across a corner of New Brunswick, and came to the Gaspé peninsula in Québec. We took a couple of days to work our way slowly around the peninsula's coastline. I loved the quaint little fishing villages and rocky seashore. At Perce Rock, a natural arch in the sea, I found I could "skip" one-foot-square pieces of slate if I twisted just so and threw them at an appropriate angle.

As we traveled through Québec, I was pleased to find that my high school Latin class enabled me to interpret French signs and brochures. I didn't know every word but could usually get the gist of it.

We took a boat to Bonaventure Island one day and walked a mile through its interior to visit a seabird sanctuary on the opposite coast. We were the only visitors on the island except for two French Canadians back at the dock waiting for the return boat. We tried to talk to one of them, a trim, elegant man in a suit, but he spoke no English.

The other man looked like a bum. He hadn't shaved in days, wore tattered clothes, and was asleep on the dock. His old shirt hung askew and his big belly moved up and down as he snored. The well-dressed man prodded the "bum" and woke him up. We found that the men were brothers traveling together, and the "bum" was actually a pleasant, bilingual, college president.

From Gaspé we drove 350 miles in one day, briefly catching the sights in Québec city and Montréal as we cruised through. We camped just inside Ontario that night and drove 550 miles to Sault Ste. Marie, Michigan the following day. We drove home from "The Soo" in a day, having traveled 4,500 miles in 21 days. This trip, our sixth summer of traveling, completed our visits to the forty-eight contiguous states and added three Canadian provinces as well.

Dear Grandkids,

I've been promising you my crow stories—tales of a wonderful pet named Sam.

He was fun and funny. Mischievous and affectionate. Smart and sassy.

I found him during my eighth-grade year. It all started with a springtime walk in the muck fields.

Love, Grandpa Glen

Glen feeding tidbits to Shadow and Sam the crow.

Chapter 12—Sam the Crow

I strolled beneath a row of black willows. These trees, planted generations ago, formed a windbreak between fields. Their new leaves were still tiny. I craned my head, searching for something interesting. My dog, Shadow, ran ahead.

Here and there, a piece of plywood or a twisted chunk of metal still stuck in upper branches. These were remnants and reminders of buildings blown away by the 1956 tornado. Some chunks stayed in treetops for decades.

Then I saw a crow nest lodged fifty feet off the ground. I scrambled up for a closer look. It wasn't easy, even for an experienced climber like myself. The crows had chosen a tree that had been blown by west winds for generations. It now leaned eastward, slightly less than straight up. The first thirty feet had no major branches.

Instead, small "sucker" branches grew in clusters along the top side of the trunk. I couldn't pull myself up by these little branches. They were too weak. I couldn't shinny over and around them. They were too thick. I climbed anyway, breaking some branches and squirming between others. The crows had shrewdly chosen a tree that protected them from nest-raiding racoons. But not from me.

I examined the nest. The crows started with a two-foot-wide platform of bigger branches. Then they kept adding smaller and finer twigs. Finally, they finished with a soft cup of dry grass. I have never seen a better-built nest.

It was beautiful but empty. I returned for another look a week later. This time my brothers came along. So did my youngest brother's friend, Harlan. I climbed again. The nest now held five eggs colored a light bluish green, speckled with cinnamon.

"Can I climb up?" my brother's friend asked. "I want to see it."

"It's difficult and dangerous," I warned. "You won't survive a fall."

"Please let me try."

"I guess you can try; let me help you."

I climbed back up and removed more sucker branches. Then I scurried down and coached Harlan step by step.

"Grab here, clutch there, scrunch past the next place," I called.

Harlan made it all the way to the nest, got a good look, and followed my coaching down again. I was pleased and proud.

"Harlan, you deserve a trophy."

Once again, I climbed all the way to the nest, took one egg, and carefully carried it down.

"Here's your trophy," I said. "If you take it home and prick pinholes in each end, you can blow the inside out and keep the shell forever."

I don't know if Harlan, the brave nest climber, still has a crow egg. I do know that he became a scientist, an important inventor, a successful businessman, and a philanthropist. I'm glad he didn't fall out of a crow tree when we were wild unsupervised children.

I returned every few days to check the nest. The eggs became baby birds. They were naked, blind, and helpless. Then they grew little pin feathers and opened their eyes. Soon, feathers covered their bodies as they grew rapidly.

They were always hungry and squawked urgently with heads held high. The baby crows acted like I was a parent bringing food. Adult crows spend springtime feeding their babies. Crows are omnivorous so both parents forage widely for anything tasty. They don't remember whose turn it is. They just keep shoving food at big, loud mouths.

I wasn't there to feed crows. I peeked quickly, climbed down, and went home. I was waiting for the babies to be the size of full-grown robins, the right size for capturing pet crows. Smaller birds have a low survival rate. Bigger ones will never be completely tame.

Finally, the time was right. I went back with my brothers, a bushel basket, and a rope. I climbed up and lowered the rope. My brothers tied the basket on. I drew it up, put the nest in, carefully lowered it, and walked home with a basket of baby crows. I'm ashamed, now, that I took the whole nest and every baby. But I was in junior-high school—a time not known for kindness and wisdom.

The world didn't change much for my baby crows. Their view had changed from treetops to a wire-mesh cage behind our garage. But they were still in their nest and still constantly hungry. They kept us busy, feeding them shredded whole-wheat bread, soaked in milk. We were their parents now.

We supplemented their food with extra water, using a ball syringe to deliver it. This feeding and watering routine had to be repeated every half hour, all day long. Sometimes we had to wait a little longer, but the crows were unhappy if we did.

My mother helped on school days and the birds thrived under our constant care. Soon they were almost full grown and walking around flapping their wings. They were getting strong, and the cage had grown too small. I decided to keep the biggest and boldest of the bunch. "Sam" would be his name.

I called a pet store and made arrangements to trade spare birds for an aquarium full of fish. This whole venture was highly illegal but nobody cared. Back then, crows could be hunted year-round without limit. Hundreds of thousands were killed for sport every year, but it was illegal (and still is) to keep a single one for a pet.

Back home, Sam got all my attention. I took him out frequently and tossed him gently up. He fluttered down, going farther each day. Sam was soon flying well, but I kept him safe in his cage most of the time. I was protecting him from the neighbors' cat.

Our next-door neighbors were Cuban refugees. Their cat was named "Babarucio," properly pronounced with a strong roll on the "r" that sounded halfway between a purr and a growl. He was coal-black, a fierce hunter who pounced on anything that moved. Babarucio paid little attention to Sam in a cage, but watched eagerly for a crow on the loose.

One day, Babarucio got his chance. Sam stood alone in the middle of the yard. Babarucio twitched with excitement and crept closer. The cat snuck behind one tree and another. Sam stared in the opposite direction—or seemed to. A crow's eyes cover almost 360 degrees. Sam stood nonchalant as Babarucio snuck ever nearer.

The cat slunk low. His tail twitched. He drew closer and closer. Sam still acted oblivious. Babarucio made his final pounce. The cat landed on bare ground. Sam had jumped and flapped his wings at the last moment. He quickly hopped just beyond Babarucio's reach.

Completely bewildered, Babarucio looked around and saw Sam a few feet away. Sam still stared in the opposite direction. Babarucio ran and pounced again. Sam flapped his wings again and hopped away. They repeated this routine several times as Sam made his way across the yard.

Now Sam stood in front of a little plywood box that had a cat-sized hole in its side. Sam looked in with a determined stare. Babarucio quivered with frustration and anticipation. Then he made his final pounce. Sam hopped to the top of the box as Babarucio's momentum carried him inside.

Babarucio turned to leave but Sam swung his sharp beak down like a pickax. Babarucio yowled and drew back. Sam waited patiently. He nailed the cat again and again until he stopped trying to escape. Then Sam flew quietly away, leaving Babarucio still afraid and still inside.

Babarucio had learned a lesson, but not his final one. Sam became an expert flier and was never caged again. He watched for Babarucio but didn't seem concerned. Then one morning (several days after the plywood box incident) came the apple tree episode.

The tree was large and poorly pruned, with many twisted branches. Sam sat on a low branch as Babarucio crept closer. Sam ignored him. Babarucio climbed the tree and worked toward Sam. Sam hopped to another branch a little higher up. The cat kept climbing and the crow kept moving higher and higher.

Finally, Sam settled on a high, odd place where an overhanging branch created a space that Babarucio could jump to but not from. Babarucio never saw it coming. He jumped up and was stuck. No place to turn. No way down. Sam flew away calling, "HAW, HAW, HAW."

Eventually, I took pity on the cat and rescued him with a ladder. This time he had learned his lesson. Babarucio, the mighty hunter, never bothered Sam again.

Dear Grandkids,

Ninth grade, and the summer before it, was a lot more fun than junior high.

I especially enjoyed spending time with Sam, my pet crow.

Love Grandpa Glen

Glen and his family when Glen was in High School.
Back row, left to right: Ross, Glen, Ellen, Bruce.
Front row: Stan, Margaret, Marian.

Chapter 13 – Ninth Grade

Just before ninth grade, I spent a week camping with Uncle Alan and Aunt Leah's family. We stayed on their forty-acre parcel near the national forest, about a mile from my present home.

This property is only accessible by foot or by a little-used, unmaintained, two-track road. It's an unusual "forty"—only 220 yards wide but half a mile long. Uncle Alan, Aunt Leah, and my younger cousins camped at the east end of their property. My cousin David and I camped on the west.

Alan's forty was an almost treeless expanse of rolling hills and valleys covered with grass and bracken ferns. David and I chose a camping spot in a little meadow near a big beaver pond. Several old apple trees grew near the center of the meadow, close to the bumpy outline of a long-gone log cabin. David and I chopped trees and sticks to build a lean-to big enough for both our sleeping bags. The front side was open and airy. We built a fire every evening, both to keep mosquitoes away and to roast apples.

We picked apples off the old trees, skewered them on sticks, and baked them over coals. We let them sizzle and caramelize until they were as tender as apple pie. They were delicious, especially to teenage boys who had been outdoors all day.

We ate our meals with the family at the other end of the property but were mostly on our own all day. We explored the Manistee National Forest, built a raft, and poled out onto the beaver pond. We stood atop a beaver lodge and watched herons feed their young in a nearby rookery.

One evening, we experienced a strange phenomenon. It was a quiet night with not a breath of wind, as far as we could tell. David and I were sitting by our campfire roasting apples when we heard his family talking. Their voices were faint at first but grew louder and clearer.

We thought they were close, maybe taking a moonlit walk. We called back but they didn't answer. We scrambled to our feet and set out to meet them. They weren't as near as we thought. We ambled across hills and valleys, still hearing clear conversation. We kept calling them but they never answered.

Finally, we topped the last hill and saw them still sitting by their campfire, right where they'd been all along. Their conversation had somehow drifted half a mile to our camp. Some subtle breeze must have flowed from them to us. We heard them clearly, but they couldn't hear us. I never experienced anything like it again.

Back home, Sam slept each night in a small, dense grove of evergreens about two city blocks from our house. He stayed there each morning until I called him, "Sam! Sam!" Then he soared up and sailed toward me at top speed. At twenty feet out, he twisted his wings and slipstreamed onto my outstretched arm.

He always looked like he was having the time of his life when he twisted from a fast glide to a gentle landing. How I wished that I could fly like a crow, especially on windy days when he enjoyed extra acrobatics.

Sam loved to tease the dog. I always fed them at the same time, giving each dry dog food—a big bowl for Shadow and a little one for Sam. Sam liked to play a mean trick on Shadow. He snuck up behind the dog and yanked his tail. Shadow whirled around while Sam flapped over his head, grabbed a bite of food, and flew off. Then he landed in an overhead tree and called, "Haw, Haw."

Sam thought this game could go on forever. He thought the dog would never wise up. He was wrong. Sam tried his trick once too often, and Shadow reared up instead of whirling around. He grabbed Sam out of the air—gently but firmly.

Perhaps Shadow had bird dog instincts after all. He put Sam on the ground and held him upside down with a paw on each wing. Nose to nose, Shadow growled and growled before letting the crow loose, unharmed. Sam treated Shadow with respect after that.

We always had a big garden, and as the oldest boy, tending it was mainly my responsibility. I took special care with sweet bell peppers, choosing the best ones for the local fair. I usually won a blue ribbon, but Sam had developed a delight in nipping little peppers. He didn't eat them, he just picked them for fun. He also pulled buds off dahlias. Sometimes I caught him and yelled "Sam!" in my most disapproving voice. Then he would stuff his loot under a plant before turning toward me with an innocent look.

Sam learned to say, "Hello." I repeated it to him; he repeated it back to me. When he had mastered a clear firm "Hello," he put it to use on a neighbor lady. She was a night owl who slept in. Sam took to early-morning visits. He tapped sharply on her door while saying, "Hello, Hello, Hello." Then he flew to a nearby tree to caw "Haw, Haw" when she answered.

Sam also had fun when I rode my bike around town. He flew from one power pole to another, waiting on each as the slow kid caught up with the fast crow. Sam even came along when I topped onions that August. He spent a little time at my side each morning but took off when the sun grew hot.

He landed in a not-too-distant row of trees—the line of black willows where he was born. There he stayed until lunch time. When I called, "Sam!" "Sam!" he rose up, sailed in, and shared my sandwich.

Soon, summer was over and I started ninth grade in our brand-new high school. The building was well-planned and well-built, but some taxpayers were outraged at its expense. They were particularly incensed that it had a swimming pool, of all things. Who needs that?

I joined the freshman football team that year—the only fall sport at my school. Lacking special skills, I was assigned a lineman's position. I had reached my adult height but still weighed less than 120 pounds. I practiced faithfully, but usually sat the bench during games.

Later that autumn, I enjoyed my first "opening day" of deer hunting. Back then, the woods were thick with hunters, many more than now. I chose a good spot to sit and wait for deer. Other hunters walked around. Still others organized large "drives" where a long line marched through the woods, pushing deer to people waiting on the edges. The deer were always stirred up and moving.

I didn't wait long. First several does strolled by, and without a doe permit, I watched them go. Then a nice six-point buck drifted in. I raised my rifle and aimed. And aimed. The more I aimed, the more my gun wobbled. My heart pounded as I finally pulled the trigger. BOOM. The buck ran off unscathed.

An hour later, another buck was standing ahead of me. Where did he come from? I carefully raised my rifle, aimed again, and wobbled again. My heart pounded and I missed. Then, several does and fawns tip-toed past. They were entertaining, but no antlers, no shot. Later, another six-pointer came sneaking my way. I raised my gun, pulled the trigger, and missed again. I had a bad case of what hunters call "buck fever."

The winter of 1963-1964 was an exciting time. Our little Dutch town was filled with tall and talented basketball players. Both high schools, Unity Christian and Hudsonville Public, had undefeated teams. When they met at regionals, the breathtaking game see-sawed back and forth. Unity sank a basket in the last second of the third overtime. They won the game and went on to place second in the state that year.

We had a problem with Sam the crow that spring. He was a friendly pet who liked to sit on my shoulder and nuzzle my ear. Then he tried it with our neighbor's preschooler. She was terrified. Her mother came over and gave my father an earful. My dad listened solemnly. "Sam has to go," he said.

I talked to Charlie and Carla, friends from school, who lived on a farm. They had many pets but would be delighted with one more.

Sam spent several years at his new home but later came to an unfortunate end. Charlie and Carla's family was less strait-laced than ours. Sam developed a colorful vocabulary which he used on a neighboring farmer. Finally, the farmer was fed up with being cussed out by a crow. Sam's adventurous life ended with a hot-tempered shotgun blast.

Shadow getting a bath.

Dear Grandkids,

Originally, I just meant to tell you about my childhood. Now, I want to tell you more.

I did better in high school than in junior high. They were fun years.

I'll tell you a little about them.

Love, Grandpa Glen

Hudsonville High School Cross Country team.
Glen is second from the right in the front row.

Chapter 14—High School Years

My school added cross-country as a new fall sport when I was a sophomore. I immediately joined the team and, to my surprise, instantly became the top runner.

My cross-country coach was actually the Junior-Varsity basketball coach. He wasn't interested in running. Pre-season conditioning for basketball players was his goal. Our team (half basketballers and half runners) ran short workouts every afternoon. My running abilities, such as they were, owed little to the coaching or training I received.

The school year flew by and summer returned. We were getting ready for an addition to our house, so we spent a short vacation on Isle Royale instead of taking a car trip. We camped at Daisy Farm Campground on Lake Superior's shore. Each day we hiked inland to Angleworm Lake, where we fished for northern pike from an unwieldy, inflatable raft. For several hours every day, my dad battled breezes, struggling to move anywhere, paddling with short, awkward oars.

I once volunteered to take a turn rowing but was worn out in a few minutes. I'm sure my dad tired just as quickly, but he never gave up. Persistence was his strong suit. That trip gave him bursitis that plagued him the rest of his life. I wish he could have said, "This is too hard," but he was never one to quit.

Later that summer, my Uncle Stanley Dahlstrom—a shop teacher in a nearby town—served as the lead builder and general contractor for our new addition. We would gain extra basement area, a spacious family room, and a "boy's dormitory" upstairs.

Our excavation contractor didn't dig the basement hole as deep as we needed. My dad decided that we boys could finish the job. We dug shovelfuls of wet sand, filled five-gallon buckets, and carried them up a ladder. We emptied our buckets and repeated the process thousands of times. Eventually the hole was deep enough.

We erected new framing while also ripping out boards where the old house and new addition met. One day, while working in tennis shoes, I stepped on a board with a nail sticking up. The nail went through my shoe and into my foot. I screamed, jumped, and landed on another board with a nail that speared my foot again.

I took driver's training later that summer and didn't do well. Most kids in the area, especially farm kids, had years of experience driving tractors and such prior to class. I had never driven anything, not even a riding lawn mower, and I barely passed the course. My instructor urged my parents to give me many hours of supervised driving over the next few months.

My dad took this to heart and had me drive him to the lumber company the next day. His constant, agitated, commentary made me more and more nervous. Still, I was okay until we got to the store and I scraped the side of the car against a telephone pole. Although my dad was upset, he let me take the driver's seat again as we drove home.

I made it home without incident and started to pull into the odd, temporary parking space in our tiny front yard.

Our usual driveway held a mound of dirt and another mound filled most of the front yard. The car barely fit in a spot that had the front porch on one side, the mailbox on the other, and a dirt pile ahead.

I started to pull into the spot when my dad decided I needed more help. He bounded out of the car and stood in front of it, waving his arms and shouting directions. I parked without trouble and had already put my foot on the brake when he threw his arms up and screamed "STOP."

I was so startled that my foot jumped off the brake and slammed onto the accelerator. The car careened into the dirt as my dad jumped away just in time. That was the end of my practice driving for a while. Finally, my patient mother gave me more time behind the wheel, and I qualified for my license on my sixteenth birthday.

After school started that fall, my friends and I decided to run for class offices. Nobody ever campaigned for these positions because the same popular kids won every time. We were less popular and never expected to win, but we had fun.

We formed a slate of four candidates for the four positions and named our slate CSVAK after our last names—Cheyne, Schilling, Van Antwerp, and Kuipers. We bought reams of colored 8.5 x 11 paper and made hundreds of hand-written posters with themes like, "Vote CSVAK" and "Up with CSVAK" and "CSVAK Forever." Then we figured a way to sneak into school after hours. We posted signs up and down hallways and placed one on every classmate's locker.

I expected that teachers and administrators would call us in for questioning, but they must have viewed it as a harmless prank. Nobody said anything.

Election day passed with the usual popular kids elected. My friend Gerry (Kuipers) later wrote in my yearbook, "For some foul reason we weren't able to seat any CSVAK member, but that's okay because nobody in their right mind would want a job like that." I think he was putting the best face on it. We would have been delighted if any of us had won.

The Spring Street house, including the addition on the left. Picture painted by artist Esther Tanis Van Allsburg, a friend of Glen's from kindergarten on.

Dear Grandkids,

My family spent a lot of time in church.

I also went to church camps and other church-related activities.

They were an important part of my upbringing.

Love, Grandpa Glen

Glen, as a twelve-year-old, at Camp Awana in front of his cabin, appropriately named Cedar.

Chapter 15 - Church, Camps, and Clubs

My family and I always attended Sunday services, both morning and evening. Midweek found us back at church for Awana club. Awana was a Christian version of Boy Scouts. Each meeting started with games followed by a time of singing Christian songs. Then we moved on to lessons, crafts, and Bible memorization.

I loved Awana. It let me compete in things I was good at. Awana was founded in the 1940s by a Chicago minister named Lance Latham. Eventually it expanded to other churches, first around Chicago and then all over the world. Camp Awana, located on a pretty lake in Wisconsin, came along shortly. I spent a week there each summer for several years as a boy.

The drive to Camp Awana took most of a day, passing through Gary, Indiana, where we choked on smog belching from factories. Then we drove through busy downtown Chicago with its endless miles of red lights and stop-and-go traffic. We followed the Lake Michigan shoreline north, wended our way through Milwaukee, and proceeded through the Wisconsin countryside to camp. I felt like we had journeyed half a world away.

I loved everything about Camp Awana. It had a hilltop bonfire ring, a freshwater spring, a stream flowing through cedar woods, and a lake. A grassy expanse held an archery golf course, tennis courts, and horizontal bars for gymnastics. Campers stayed in small rustic cabins and ate in a large dining hall.

Lance "Doc" Latham, the camp director, was an inspiring figure. He was past retirement age, and looked it, with his white hair and deeply-creased face.

But he was youthful in body and spirit—a loving and well-loved man.

Lance had been a child prodigy, the son of a Pennsylvania Presbyterian minister who was determined to maximize his son's giftedness. Lance started piano lessons at age three and could soon play any song in the hymnbook by memory,

He also memorized Bible passages daily, learning several books of the Bible by age seven. He studied Latin and Greek, graduated from college at age 17, picked up a Master's Degree in Biochemistry, and further developed his musical training at the Philadelphia Conservatory.

Lance Latham was a man of many talents—he was even an accomplished athlete in several sports—but he was humble and kind. I, like other campers, admired him greatly. I once won an "All Around Pal" award and was proud when he presented it to me.

Later, I attended Lake Ann Bible Camp near Traverse City, Michigan. It was closer to home and it had girls. I was quickly attracted to a preacher's pretty daughter. We later wrote letters and found opportunities to visit for several months—my first teenage romance.

In high school, I competed on a Bible quiz team sponsored by Youth for Christ. The concept seemed normal at the time but now strikes me as odd. YFC quizzes emphasized scripture memorization. Moderators asked questions and contestants jumped up to answer them. Chairs were wired with pads to show who jumped first. We earned or lost points for correct or incorrect answers. Each quiz season focused on a particular book of the Bible, so I memorized the book of Jonah the year it was the topic.

Quiz tournaments featured local teams vying to advance to regional and national levels. I remember exciting tournaments, but I don't remember any deeper discussion about scripture. We were there to memorize words, not to understand Biblical themes or applications.

Still, I'm glad that I memorized Jonah. I identify with him. God told him to do something. He said, "No." God persisted. He still said, "No." God upped the ante. Jonah sullenly and reluctantly complied. That theme runs through my life, too. I have lived through many Jonah times when my obedience to God's promptings have been slow, reluctant, and grudging.

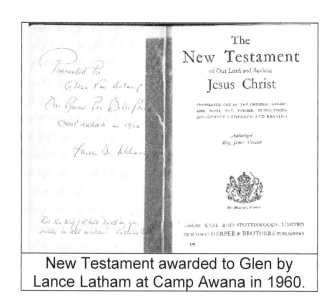

New Testament awarded to Glen by Lance Latham at Camp Awana in 1960.

Dear Grandkids,

My family drove to Alaska for vacation just before my Senior year of high school.

It was the longest and best of our camping trips.

I'm just glad I wasn't mauled by a grizzly bear. Aren't you?

> *Love, Grandpa Glen*

Stan Van Antwerp's picture of Mt. McKinley (Denali) reflecting in Wonder Lake.

Chapter 16 – Alaska Trip

The summer before my Senior year of high school, we took a trip to Alaska. It was a great adventure, the crowning highlight of all our summer vacations. We left on a Friday evening, after my dad was out of work, and drove two hours to Ludington. There we caught the ferry across Lake Michigan to Manitowoc, Wisconsin. It departed around 8 p.m. and arrived near midnight. We had sleeping berths to catch some rest before driving through the night.

My dad drove across Wisconsin. By midmorning we were deep into Minnesota and stopped to share brunch with friends there. My dad, my mother, and I took turns as we drove on. We crossed Minnesota, much of North Dakota, and turned north into Saskatchewan. From Friday evening to Saturday evening, we had covered more than 1,000 miles plus a four-hour ferry ride.

After church in Saskatoon Sunday morning, we continued west across Canadian prairies. Endless wheat fields created unobstructed horizons as we watched small towns with tall grain elevators fade behind and grow ahead.

Finally, we came to Alberta and made our way to the magnificent Canadian national parks at Banff and Jasper. I was enchanted by their beautiful rugged mountains and deep sparkling lakes. We spent a couple of days wandering through these parks. Just five days after leaving home, we came to Dawson Creek, British Columbia—the start of the Alaska-Canadian Highway.

We were delighted that the Alaska highway was well maintained. Although entirely gravel, it was graded constantly and we motored along at a steady fifty-miles-per-hour. The scenery was beautiful, especially mountainsides that were covered with brilliant blooming fireweed.

Once, we stopped for a picnic lunch near a bridge that spanned a little creek. My brothers and I decided to explore the stream after we ate. We walked along it until we came to the majestic Yukon River, our first glimpse of it on this trip. I was amazed at how broad and vast this untamed river was.

Later we stopped at another creek and went fishing. Bruce caught a good-sized grayling, and I caught an even bigger Dolly Varden trout. I didn't have a net so I yanked it out of the water by hand. We had a nice fish supper that evening.

On our way to Alaska we took a side trip through Dawson, a gold-mining village from the late 1890s. It's the place where Jack London and Robert Service lived and wrote during gold rush days. There we met an old miner called Black Mike. Although he was well over 90 years old, his bushy beard was still black and his mind was still sharp. I sat in rapt attention as he told stories of gold-mining days.

We continued on towards Alaska, crossed high country near the border, and stopped to watch a family of ptarmigan. These beautiful, grouse-like birds (who were quite tame) gave us a close-up view. They were not used to seeing people and were as curious about us as we were about them.

In Alaska we met paved roads again but it actually slowed us down. Annual freeze-thaw cycles had buckled the pavement. The paved roads were less level than the well-graded gravel highways we had been traveling.

The people in Alaska were extremely friendly. One evening, as we unloaded the car-top carrier and pitched the tent, another camper wandered over.

"Have you ever had caribou?" he asked.

"Never," said my dad.

"I shot one last fall and have steaks in my cooler. Would you like some?"

"We certainly would!"

The man, a complete stranger, grilled steaks for our entire family.

My mother had second cousins who lived near Anchorage in a house on a little lake. We stayed with them a night or two and swam at 11 o'clock each evening in a lake as warm as a bathtub—hardly what we expected in Alaska.

We drove down the Kenai Peninsula and fished for salmon in Resurrection Creek. Catching more than enough for supper, we went to a cannery and exchanged our surplus fish for canned salmon that we took home to enjoy later.

We were in Alaska during a heat wave. It was nearly one hundred degrees when we went to church on a Sunday morning in Fairbanks. The church threw their doors and windows open as they had no other air-conditioning.

We drove up to Mount McKinley National Park, now called Denali. At that time everyone could drive private cars all the way through the park. We saw lots of wildlife. At Cathedral Mountain we parked, hiked uphill, and watched mountain goats near the top where I worked my way around a cliff and spotted them from twenty feet away. I was thrilled and decided to run back down the mountain. Halfway down, as I barged through a willow thicket, a bull Caribou with tall branching antlers jumped up and ran off.

We drove on and in less than a mile saw a sow grizzly bear with twin cubs. Suddenly, it occurred to me that I had been foolish bursting through a willow thicket. Seeing a caribou was thrilling. I could have met grizzlies just as easily. That would have been a different story.

We hit Mount McKinley at a perfect time. We met a photographer couple who had spent a week at Wonder Lake Campground, waiting for a good view of the mountain. The clouds cleared as we joined them, and it stayed clear until we left two days later. It was light enough for reading around the clock, with twilight persisting from sunset to sunrise.

Reluctantly we left beautiful Alaska, and again we made good time down the Alaska Highway. Then we crossed the prairie provinces and Ontario, traveling 2100 miles to reach Michigan at Sault Ste. Marie in four days. Another day of just 300 miles, with stops to see relatives along the way, took us home. It had been a gorgeous trip, one we would all remember the rest of our lives.

A short time later, during a cool spell back in Michigan, we went swimming at a small lake. It was almost too cold to go in the water. A friend said I must have frozen in Alaska if it was this cold in Michigan. I laughed and told about swimming in bathtub-warm waters under the midnight sun.

Marvelous Alaskan scenery near Denali. Picture taken by Glen on his recent trip to Alaska.

Dear Grandkids,

Your Grandmother and I have always enjoyed teenagers. We had lots of fun with your parents when they were that age. We enjoyed their personalities, their friends, and their humor.

Now, five of you (soon to be six) are teenagers as well, and we are enjoying these years with you.

However, there are two scary times for a parent (or grandparent) of teens. The first is new-driver time. The second is starting college. Both times are especially dangerous—in very different ways.

Four of you have made, or are making the first transition. Two have made the second. You seem to be doing well.

We pray for you every day.

> *Love, Grandpa Glen*

Glen's High School
graduation picture.

Chapter 17 - Senior Year

After our Alaska trip, summer lasted another six weeks. I worked in an onion-packing plant—hard, dirty work that paid well. I enjoyed working with a high school friend as well as a group of young "Mexican" men. Once, on a dare, I took a bite of Pedro's lunchtime burrito. His food was so hot that even fellow Hispanics wouldn't touch it. My mouth burned for an hour.

September came and I began my last year of high school. Cross-country practices and meets occupied my time and attention. I was still the fastest runner on the team, or almost the fastest. My friend Dave, a grade behind me, had improved greatly. He often matched my pace in practice and even ran faster sometimes.

Dave lived eight miles south of town on a family apple orchard. I worked there during the harvest, hitchhiking back and forth each Saturday. I loved the crisp fall days and Golden Delicious apples fresh off the tree. One Saturday evening, after a long day picking apples, Dave suggested, "Let's run to Hudsonville. I'll call my dad to drive me home."

"It's eight miles," I snorted. "We can't run that far."

"I think we can," Dave calmly replied.

"We never run that far, not even close."

"I'm going to do it," Dave said. "It's your choice to come along or not."

"Okay, I'll give it a try."

We started jogging at a steady pace. After several miles without a break, I gasped, "Let's walk a little and then run again."

"I'll keep going, stop if you want."

"Okay, I'll run a bit more."

We kept jogging and eventually fell into a steady rhythm. I felt strong as we passed the five, six, and seven-mile marks. I was still surprisingly fresh when we reached Hudsonville. Dave collapsed on the curb and sat for several minutes before staggering to his feet again.

Dave's persistence made my senior season special. I learned that I was faster and tougher than I imagined. I became a top runner in my league, trading best weekly times with a couple runners from other schools.

The Lowell Invitational in Fallasburg Park was a memorable race. Dozens of schools from the greater Grand Rapids area competed. Hundreds of runners stood shoulder to shoulder, waiting for the starting pistol. The gun sounded and I sprinted at top speed to reach a sharp turn one hundred yards out.

I briefly slipped and fell as the pack jostled and bumped each other at the turn. I scrambled to my feet and ran a good race. At the finish, a fellow racer pointed at my foot and asked, "When did you get spiked?"

I glanced down in surprise and saw my foot bleeding in three spots. Apparently, a runner in racing spikes ran over my foot as I slipped at the opening turn. I was so focused on the race that I never noticed.

My injuries weren't serious and healed quickly. I continued to have a good season and soon my coach was asking, "Do you want to go to regional and state meets."

He looked hopeful that I'd decline. I was his only qualifying runner. His responsibilities as coach would end if I said no.

I thought about the coming cold weather and decided to call it quits for the season. I later found that I could have finished among the top runners. Other runners whose times matched mine earned invitations to run for Michigan State University.

Meanwhile, the deadline for SATs loomed and I was among the last Seniors to ask for an application. The high school counselor, a teacher overdue for retirement, shuffled through his desk and handed me a form. I filled it out and mailed it in. Soon I received notice that my test time and place would be in Indian River (a tiny town near the straits of Mackinaw) on deer season's opening weekend.

I knew that my classmates were taking the SAT in a town close to home. I was mad at myself for filing so late and drawing an inconvenient time and place. As usual, I kept my feelings to myself and chose to skip the test. I didn't know this would disqualify me from being a National Merit Finalist.

My high school counselor came to me months later and asked why I hadn't taken the test. When I told him about my problems with the time and place, he had a surprising response. "I ran out of forms, so I used last year's for four students. That caused the problem. One student came to me and I fixed it." He never said why he didn't fix it for the rest of us.

Deer season came and my friend Dave went north with me to hunt on my grandfather's farm near Cadillac. I borrowed my sister Ellen's new Plymouth Valiant. Dave and I had a great time riding and hunting together, even though we didn't get deer.

We drove home after dark on a busy two-lane highway that wound through open countryside and little towns south of Big Rapids. I drove fast and passed other cars continually. Suddenly, my right front tire exploded with a loud bang and a sudden lurch. I couldn't control the car. It swerved back and forth from one lane to the other. I struggled to slow down and keep on the road.

We must have had a guardian angel on board—we missed every car as we veered wildly in and out of oncoming traffic. We narrowly missed several sixty-mile-per-hour head-on collisions before we pulled onto the shoulder and changed the tire. The rest of our drive was slow and uneventful.

The highlight of my Senior year was a journalism class where I was one of a dozen students who wrote and produced a weekly school newspaper. Our sponsor was an English teacher whose supervision was light. I had lots of time to roam the halls.

I found that I often went to the library where our new exchange student had study hall. I had never dated anyone from my own town because I was prejudiced. More than ninety percent of the kids my age were of Dutch descent. Even though they were friendly, I thought they secretly considered me an outsider. Now, here was a Scandinavian girl, more an outsider than I could ever be.

I was fascinated and became her friend and then her boyfriend. I fell deeply, hopelessly in love and built unrealistic expectations that we could somehow survive an eventual across-the-ocean relationship.

After the SAT debacle, I decided I didn't want to attend college anyway. Again, I decided this in my own mind and didn't discuss it with anyone. Eventually, my high school principle called me to his office and said, "I'm reviewing college applications and I don't see anything for you."

"I decided not to go."

"Why not?"

"Because there's nothing I want to study."

"You seem to enjoy journalism," he said as he furrowed his brow and leaned forward. "Why don't you study that?"

"Well, maybe."

"Michigan State University has a fine Journalism school. Why don't you apply?"

He gradually talked me into the idea and helped me start my application. Soon I found that I was accepted at MSU, into the Honors College as well as the Journalism School.

I was involved in a less than honorable incident a few days later while eating lunch in the cafeteria. A kid named Keith, who had been in my class since kindergarten, finished a banana and threw the peel backwards. It sailed over several tables and hit my head.

I stood up, grabbed the peel, and saw Keith laughing with his friends. I wadded the peel and threw it back as I called, "Did you lose this, Keith?"

The peel smacked Keith in the face. Every student in the room silently stared at the unfolding drama. Keith stormed over and started pummeling me with his fists. I was five feet, eight inches tall—thin and wiry. Keith was well over six feet, and much heavier than me. But I was fast. I dodged and got his back against the table. Then I slammed into his chest. His knees buckled as he fell on his back.

I figured I had won the fight and made my point. I growled, "Leave me alone" and let Keith up. Big mistake. He started pounding me again until teachers poured into the cafeteria and broke it up. Both Keith and I got several days of detention for ungentlemanly behavior.

My American History teacher that year was a rigid lady named Mrs. D. She used lesson plans that never varied from year to year. Snow days upset her because she had to adjust. She didn't like adjusting.

She also served as gym teacher for the girls. She believed strongly in effort, but my commitment to it didn't match her standards. I loved American History and had been reading about it since grade school. Since the textbook offered a quick, easily-absorbed summary, I breezed through the chapters and called it good.

Mrs. D's grading system was based on quizzes and tests. Each quiz or test had extra credit questions. A student could score above 100% by answering everything correctly. I always did. Our textbook also included end of chapter questions that we could answer in writing for additional extra credit. I never bothered.

I received an A+ for the first two marking periods with no apparent effort. Mrs. D didn't like it. She made the written questions a requirement. I saw no point in doing them so she kept lowering my grade. I continued to get an A+ on tests, but my final grade declined to a B+ and then a B before reaching a B- in the final period. The school year, and my standoff with Mrs. D came to an end.

After graduation, my girlfriend went back to Finland. But first, she broke off our relationship. She realized that a long-distance romance would not work. I was crushed.

Glen at high school graduation with his foreign exchange student girlfriend.

Dear Grandkids,

When I was in college, my friends and I were very optimistic. We thought we could change the world. We thought we would. Our musical heroes sang about love and peace. We practiced tolerance and brotherhood.

The Viet Nam War ended, but the world didn't change much. Even our musicians found it hard to get along with their own band members. Our hopes faded.

I think the present generation is a mirror image of mine. Hopelessness and despair are too prevalent. Too many young people think things are bad and won't get better.

Don't despair. Keep an even keel. Long-term consequences are rarely as bad, or as good, as they could be. Our best hopes may be dashed, but our worst-fears may prove groundless.

Keep the faith. God is the God of history. He grants people great autonomy but always has the final say. The world spins out of our control, but it is never out of His care.

Love, Grandpa Glen

Glen as a college freshman at Michigan State University.

Chapter 18 - College Freshman

Our family did not travel in 1967. Instead, I spent the summer working at the factory where my dad was Chief Electrical Engineer. I was one of several college students dismantling old electrical transformers for refurbishing. I earned good wages that I needed for college, having no scholarship and no help from my parents. Back then, working part time for the school year and full time all summer paid MSU's full expenses.

The summer flew by and I soon found myself at Michigan State University's freshman orientation, including "mixers" or evening dances. I didn't dance well but was enthusiastic and tireless. College was going to be fun if I didn't let classes interfere much.

I ran into two guys I raced against in high school. They were both on MSU's Cross-Country team and were surprised that I was not. They took me to the coach and introduced me. "This is Glen. He's a good runner."

"Go get a physical and come back," he said.

When I returned, he lit into me: "Running is hard. You can't just stroll in here and make the team."

"That's OK, "I answered. "I can prove myself."

He smelled like he'd been drinking and started ranting, "Go get a haircut. No hippies on my team. Is that perfectly clear?"

"Yes, it is." I walked out and never came back.

Later I learned that he pushed everyone. Some could take it. Some couldn't. Tough luck. He wasn't the right coach for me. I needed encouragement—not exactly his style.

Soon I saw a hint of my potential. MSU held an intramural one-mile run called the "Turkey Trot," each fall. Any non-varsity athlete could compete, and the first three finishers each won a live turkey. At the appointed time, I lined up beside Gary, a record-setter from my high-school conference. He graduated a year ahead of me and had run his freshman year at MSU. He became discouraged and quit several weeks into his sophomore season.

"Hi Glen," Gary said. "Glad to see you. I'll probably be slow; I haven't trained for two weeks."

"Weeks?" I thought. "I haven't trained for months."

Actually, compared to Gary, I never trained at all. I was running on sheer talent and determination. Apparently, that was enough. I took third—ahead of Gary—but behind two grad students who had run for State all their undergraduate years. I was surprised to do so well. I wondered then, and still wonder now, what I could have done if I hadn't been too proud to run for that coach.

I went back to my dorm with a grin on my face and a turkey under my arm. A friend bought it, stuffed it into a duffle bag, hitchhiked home, and enjoyed it with his family on Thanksgiving.

At the Thanksgiving break I went home myself for the first time in three months. I hitchhiked to the center of Hudsonville and walked home. My dad met me at the door with fury on his face.

"You're not coming into my house with long hair," he said.

"Okay," I said quietly as I turned to leave.

My mother flew to the door, more furious than my father. But she was furious at him, not me. He was as surprised as I was and timidly changed his mind. My mom, unlike my dad, understood other people's emotions. She knew that my quiet okay meant I would turn around and never come back.

Hair length was a big deal back then, a sign of the difference between generations. My father and his generation had served in World War II. The whole country pulled together then. Patriotism ruled. Everyone did what needed to be done.

My father didn't sense that Vietnam was different. It dragged aimlessly on with no end in sight. I felt the war was foolish and wanted no part of it. People like me wore long hair as a symbol of being against the war. To my father, this was a slap in the face. Rejecting his service. Refusing my duty. He didn't see a difference between his war and mine.

I also met with unexpected conflict in my Journalism class that fall. The professor assigned a lengthy research paper, a big part of the course grade. I wrote about San Francisco's Haight-Ashbury district and its media coverage. I criticized journalistic sensationalism.

I researched and wrote well. I expected a good grade, but my instructor gave me a 2.0 on a 4-point scale. He didn't criticize my writing or research, but he objected to my topic. I changed my mind about journalism, expecting future editors to be like my professor. Once again, proud and defiant, I walked away. Nobody would push me around.

My grades were mixed and mediocre that term. I loved my Honors college classes and did well in them. I had less interest in other classes and was content with 3.0 grades. I was more interested in socializing, both in and out of class.

During the winter term I was even more social and rarely studied, with the exception of mid-term and final exam weeks. Those were times when everybody studied and nobody noticed that I hit the books, too. I did very well on exams and aced most of my classes.

"I knew you could do it," my dad said when he saw my grades. "You just needed to try."

About that time, I met Diana. I knew her by sight—the pretty girl with long blonde hair who took tickets in the cafeteria—but I never dared introduce myself. Then I saw her siting with people I knew in our dorm-complex coffee shop. I went up and said, "Hi."

"Hi," she replied coldly as she stood up and walked away. No problem. Now that I'd met her, I stopped to chat every time we saw each other. We soon became inseparable and spent all our spare time together. My grades took another nosedive.

Dear Grandkids,

I hope you make better use of your time in college than I did with mine.

Here's the story of the rest of my college years.

Love, Grandpa Glen

Glen and Diana.

Chapter 19 – The Rest of My College Years

I bought a car in the spring of 1968 from Grandpa and Grandma Dahlstrom. Grandpa was suffering from dementia and could no longer drive. Their 1954 Chevy still ran well even though it had 100,000 miles on it—lots of miles for a car in those days. I paid my grandparents $100, equal to $740 in 2020. It was a big expense for a poor college student, but I was thrilled to have my own wheels. I hitchhiked no longer.

That summer, I worked a variety of jobs, starting with my old summer job at my dad's employer. Then an acquaintance helped me land higher-paying work at a cardboard factory in Grand Rapids. It was hot, hard, and dirty. A couple weeks was all I could take.

Next, I answered an ad for encyclopedia sales. An older fellow in his late 20's drove a carload of young people to little towns in southern Michigan. There he dropped us off in different parts of a village. We went door to door with sales literature—selling inferior and overpriced encyclopedias on installment plans.

I worked two weeks and didn't make a sale. Then I met a receptive couple who had a new baby, their first child. "Encyclopedias are great for kids," I told them. "My family had them when I was young and I learned lots from them."

"We'll buy them," they replied.

Then the husband asked his wife for their stack of bills. What could they postpone? The down payment for their encyclopedias was due immediately, but they didn't have the money. My happiness at finally making a sale disappeared.

"You don't need encyclopedias yet," I said as I tore up their contract. "Keep your money and pay your bills."

That very evening, I met a guy who had worked for the same outfit a year earlier. He told me that most of the villages where we worked had anti-peddler ordinances. Sometimes salespeople were arrested. I took his warning seriously and quit.

Next, I heard that Oldsmobile was hiring in Lansing and soon landed an assembly-line job. It was fast-paced and demanding work, but the hourly rate was fantastic. I needed every dollar to make up for the previous weeks with no pay.

Two weeks after starting, I lost the job—just when I had mastered it. A relief worker, the guy who covered for me while I was on break, let several cars slide by without parts. The foreman insisted that I had done it. He fired me on the spot. I think he expected me to fail on my own, but since I didn't, asked the relief guy to miss some cars. They probably hated my hair.

A little later I landed a job sorting used textbooks for a bookstore near MSU. Then I transitioned to my old job as a janitor on campus. I had worked six different jobs in one summer while also missing several weeks of work. I barely met fall expenses.

Meanwhile, I spent each summer weekend in Flint, staying with my friend Ron. He was an engineering student at General Motors Institute—a year-around work/study college program that led directly to engineering careers with the company. Ron shared his apartment with other GMI college kids. I crashed on their couch each night and drove across town to visit Diana daily.

Then my old car had engine problems. Ron and I spent a whole Saturday fixing it, only to have a worse blow up the next day. I became a hitchhiker again as the Chevy went to the junkyard.

Once I got a ride with someone too drunk to drive. He finally pulled over and let me take the wheel. He had mentioned that he was meeting friends at a certain bar in a town on my way. I drove him there, went into the bar, got his friends, and left him in their care while I hitched away.

That fall I moved to Campus View Apartments with several friends. I had enough money for rent and tuition but nothing more. MSU had revised its tuition schedule and used a sliding scale based on family income. I had to pay a high rate because my dad had a high salary. It didn't matter that I was financially independent and paying my own way.

I barely made it through fall term. I took to eating only one meal a day, a bowl of white rice. Sometimes Diana smuggled rolls from her dorm cafeteria, providing welcome calories.

I made a few changes over Christmas break. First, my parents agreed to pay the difference between my income and theirs on MSU's scale. Then I sold my deer rifle and coin collections. This gave me enough money to attend school, pay for my apartment, and eat healthy meals every day.

I was still going to church each Sunday. Diana went with me, but we were both drifting farther from our faith. I especially loved marijuana back then. I thought it hypocritical that the government permitted harmful alcoholic beverages but banned marijuana. We didn't talk about drug use at church.

I proposed to Diana on Valentine's Day in 1969. She and I, with four friends, squeezed into my friend Ed's two-seater MGB sportscar. We drove down to Wilcox's Second Hand Store in Lansing and found a nice diamond ring that she still wears today.

We were married on Friday the thirteenth of June, 1969. We had a simple ceremony followed by an inexpensive cake-and-ice-cream reception in the church basement. Diana's parents paid for it with cash borrowed from a paid-up life insurance policy. They had taken it out on Diana when she was a child. They gave us the policy. We could pay the borrowed money back and keep the policy or let it lapse and keep the cash. We were young and invincible. We kept the cash. Diana's cautious dad was disappointed with our choice.

I got a conventional haircut and shaved my beard for the wedding. My dad decided to protest anyway. He got a buzz cut, a shorter style than he ever wore, and demanded that my younger brother Ross get a haircut. My friend Ron said that he would take care of it. We went back to his apartment, where he made a great show of arranging his barber setup. When Ross sat down, Ron lifted a single hair, snipped it, and proclaimed, "Now you've had A Hair Cut." Back at church my dad huffed, "Better, anyway."

We borrowed an old Chevy from Diana's parents and enjoyed a brief inexpensive honeymoon at the Straits of Mackinaw. A week after our wedding, we attended the wedding of our friends Ed and Debbie. Their well-to-do Detroit families threw a strikingly extravagant ceremony and reception. The treasure chest crafted from fresh fruit, filled to overflowing with more fresh fruit, was especially impressive. Ed and Debbie spent several weeks in Europe for their honeymoon. Our differing social classes didn't affect our deep friendship.

We bought the old Chevy from Diana's parents and rented a tiny, inexpensive apartment in Flint. I landed a well-paying job at a warehouse and built strong muscles unloading boxcars. Life was good.

Young people with long hair who smoked marijuana were called "hippies." But we called ourselves "freaks." We met a group of Flint factory freaks and hung out with them in our spare time.

Meanwhile, an Indian sitar sat in a corner of our apartment—a unique wedding present. We didn't want it. Neither of us could play instruments and it gave us the creeps. A musical friend from Flint came to mind. Trouble was he had moved to Ann Arbor, and we had no way to contact him. We took the sitar and drove to Ann Arbor anyway. I felt an urge to park at a certain corner. We cut across The Quad, and found our friend sitting under a tree. We handed him the sitar, walking away with heartfelt relief.

We moved to Lansing before school started that fall, renting a charming apartment for $85 a month. It was part of an old brick house in an historic neighborhood. The Grand River made a wide bend behind our house. All houses in our two-block stretch had big backyards and gardens. A strip of untamed land lined the riverbank—a touch of country in the heart of the city. We would live there for the next ten years.

I again worked my janitor job at MSU that fall. We both enrolled in classes and Diana studied diligently. She looked forward to graduation and a teaching degree. I studied less diligently and was quite caught up in campus anti-war demonstrations.

We took a bus trip, along with hundreds of other MSU people, to our nation's capital in November for "The Moratorium to End the War." Summer had lingered and I still wore sandals with no socks when we left. Winter moved in before we reached Washington and my feet were freezing. Someone offered me spare socks that I gratefully added to my footwear.

That moratorium was the biggest gathering of people in our nation's history. A half-million protestors demanded an end to the fighting. We joined many others for free soup suppers at a downtown church. We also slept on the floor there. Once, people came in from an encounter with police. Tear-gas fumes still wafted from their clothing, making our eyes burn too.

Later that autumn, the Selective Service enacted a lottery system. Birthdates were assigned a number from 1-366. The lowest numbers would be drafted first. The highest numbers wouldn't be drafted at all. I was sure, or almost sure, that I would get a high number. I stopped going to classes but didn't quit school yet, just in case. My birthdate landed at number 342 when the lottery happened. No draft for me.

As the next term started, I decided not to attend. I thought we would save on tuition. Diana would press on and graduate while I took a break. My education could continue sometime later. I would lose my student job but expected to find better work with better pay soon.

A co-worker, a kindly graduate student from India named Jagdish, tried to persuade me to stay in school and keep my job. "Take the minimum class load," he advised. "You'll earn more than your classes cost."

I decided against it and dropped out anyway. Big mistake. I didn't find another job for three months—the whole term. We survived on a loan from my kindly friend, Jagdish. Finally, I found good-paying work as a night janitor at Meijer—a big grocery and department store. I gratefully repaid my friend.

Anti-war protests continued on campus during the spring of 1970 but we didn't attend many. We lived across town and I was working nights. Diana was student teaching in Eaton Rapids, a town twenty miles away.

Dear Grandkids,

Several doctors recently recommended medical marijuana for the nausea I get from chemotherapy.

I'll avoid it if I can. I'd rather use something else. I like being clear-headed.

Once upon a time, I used way too much marijuana. I'm glad those days are behind me and I don't want to go back.

Love, Grandpa Glen

Our teepe tent made from an old Parachute.

Chapter 20 – After College

I wrecked our car in the spring of 1970. The accident wasn't entirely my fault; the car ahead of me lacked brake lights and stopped abruptly, but I got the ticket. Our old Chevy was too damaged to repair, so we were hitchhikers again. Diana rode to school with a fellow student teacher.

Diana's good work student teaching gained her full-time employment the following year. We were thrilled and splurged on a car, a brand-new Toyota Corolla. Purchased for $2,000 on a monthly payment plan, it cost a lot of money. We loved that Corolla. It was fun, speedy, and got great gas mileage.

We made plans to take a camping trip west with our friends Ed and Debbie. We would drive our new Toyota since their MGB was way too small. We made tepee-like tents from army-surplus parachutes. They looked impressive and people asked if they were waterproof. "They're nylon," we confidently replied. "They'll shed water like a duck's back."

The day came when we packed everything in the car, making it fit somehow, and headed west. Our first stop was at a family-run campground in Iowa where the owners' teenage son admired our tepees. We were proud owners of unique accommodations.

Several horseback riders passed by as we set up camp outside Cody, Wyoming. One stopped and said, "There's lots of cowboys here who don't care for hair."

"Thanks for telling us," I replied. "We're passing through and will leave tomorrow."

We pitched one tent and shared it, sleeping well until 2 a.m. Then we awoke to waist-high flames surrounding us. Gunshots echoed nearby. Someone wanted us to leave—now! We lay still until the circle of fire, poured and ignited gasoline, faded away. Eventually, we slept again before leaving at dawn.

We passed through Yellowstone and made our way to Glacier National Park, enjoying clear, dry weather every day. A small rustic campground near an Indian reservation served us well for a week. A Blackfoot Indian family camped nearby and admired our tents. Many freaks from all over the country shared the campground with us.

One night we witnessed both a lunar eclipse and Northern Lights. It was a beautiful show in that dry mountain air.

When it was time to head home, we took turns driving night and day. We pushed through to Wisconsin and camped at a lovely lakeside National Forest campground. It would be a good place to rest for a couple of days.

The first rain of our trip started after midnight. A fine mist drifted through the tent and grew to big drops. The walls became saturated, sagged under their weight, and collapsed the tepee. Parachute nylon, we learned, is loosely woven to withstand shock—not tightly woven to repel water. We struggled out, stuffed our wet gear in the car, and took off. Driving that night and another day brought us home by evening, after dropping Ed and Debbie in Detroit.

I went back to work at Meijer. September arrived and Di taught full-time, working days while I worked nights. In the evenings, she graded papers and prepared lessons. Having little time together was hard for us, so I decided leave my job and find daytime employment. I should have done it the other way around. My search was unsuccessful and I entered a long jobless stretch. Diana's parents were never very fond of me. Now they liked me even less. They figured I was a worthless bum sponging off their hard-working daughter.

At Christmas time, a middle-aged plumber in his heavily-loaded pickup truck ran a red light and smashed our lovely Toyota. Diana went to the Emergency Room by ambulance. There she was treated for shock. A skilled surgeon removed glass shards from her face as she kept asking, "Where's my husband, is he okay?"

I remained at the accident site as a police officer asked the plumber and me about the wreck. "I had a green light and this guy ran into me," the plumber confidently stated.

I gave my story, "I had a green light and watched it carefully as I approached the four-lane cross street. One vehicle at the head of the line took off and blasted through the intersection ahead of me. The other driver, probably never looking up, hit me broadside."

"Witnesses in other cars confirmed Mr. Van Antwerp's story," the cop told the plumber. "You get a ticket for failure to yield the right of way."

"Ticket! He hit me!"

"You're not listening," I answered irately. "You ran a red light, wrecked my brand-new car, and sent my wife to the hospital."

"Well, if you think that's how it happened, what about the car that went first."

The officer shook his head and answered for me. "We would have ticketed him if we had seen him, but we didn't. You still get your ticket."

The plumber was unconvinced and took his case to court, dropping it just before trial. The evidence against him was overwhelming.

His insurance company balked at paying our full claim. "What's a Toyota?" the agent asked. "Who wants a little foreign car? I can't pay full price for that!"

In the end, we negotiated a deal where they paid what we still owed for the car but no more. I bought an ancient Renault Dauphine, a little foreign car that even I didn't want.

I was struggling deeply with my faith at that time. I had wandered far from Christian beliefs and practices. I realized that I could no longer consider myself a Christian. Jesus was certainly not my Lord. Could I still consider Him my Savior? I felt God tugging at my heart and finally gave in. I would turn my life over to God and see where He brought me.

I hadn't read the Bible at all—not for a long time. Now it was sweet and new. I read and prayed every day. I was flooded with joy. I gave up marijuana. I had grown withdrawn, depressed, and paranoid. Now I felt free.

I got a job janitoring at Meijer again. My boss couldn't believe I was the same person. Instead of being sullen and quiet, I was outgoing and happy. I was appointed the night-shift union steward.

We decided we needed a baby and were soon expecting our first child. My relationship with my dad improved as we made plans to build a canoe to take to Isle Royale together. I worked on it for months while he helped with design work. It became a beautiful craft. "I'm so proud of you," my dad boasted. "You did better than anybody else could."

I went through a succession of blue-collar jobs—installing roofing and siding, working for an antique furniture stripping shop, and more janitor work. Jeremy was born and Diana stayed home with him. Her one year of teaching would be her only full-time job for years to come.

God usually speaks to me through the Bible, pastor's sermons, or through conversations with other believers. Sometimes he also speaks more directly. I hear a still, small voice, a growing impression inside me that never wavers or fades. It grows stronger and more insistent, especially if I fight it.

I felt a leading to go to University Reformed Church, an on-campus ministry which met in the MSU Chapel. I had never been there. I hadn't attended church for years and was afraid to go. God kept pushing while I kept resisting. Eventually, I gave in a little. I left home on a Sunday morning and walked to the main thoroughfare to hitch a ride (our car had quit working).

"I'm running late," I argued with God, "and I'm not going if I can't get a ride."

The first car stopped and took me all the way to the chapel's front door. Just then, another car pulled up and parked. A young couple stepped out. I looked rather wild with my gold-rimmed glasses, hair to the middle of my back, and bushy beard, but this couple looked like my kind of people. The guy's beard and hair were bushier than mine, and they wore embroidered peasant shirts.

"I haven't been to church in years," I said as I walked up. "I'm kind of nervous. May I sit with you?"

"Sure," they replied as we walked in and took our seats. The opening hymn ended and the pastor said, "Please take a moment to introduce yourself to those around you."

"I'm Lisa," the young lady said. "Who are you?"

"Glen."

"Where are you from, Glen?"

"Lansing."

"Originally?"

"No, I grew up in a little town on the west side of the state."

"Which town?"

"Hudsonville."

"Do you know my friend, Bruce Van Antwerp?" Lisa asked.

"He's my brother," I replied.

Silently I said. "Okay God, you win. Thanks for bringing me to this church."

Diana and Jeremy soon attended with me and University Reformed Church became our beloved home and church family.

By then, I worked as an evening janitor at the Catholic Hospital in Lansing, and I loved it. I did my work well, enjoyed visiting with people, and appreciated the exercise. The near-minimum wage met our needs and more. One payday a month covered rent, another covered utilities and gasoline, one covered food, and the fourth went into savings.

It was good enough for me but wasn't good enough for my friend, Louise. "Apply at MSU if you want to be a janitor," she argued. "At least they pay better."

She kept hounding me until I gave in and made a trip to the MSU employment office. My hair was shorter then and I was clean-shaven—I looked quite presentable. The employment director, a Mr. Bachus, invited me into his office and scanned my application before asking, "Why do you want to be a janitor?"

"I have lots of experience and I love the work."

"Sorry," he said. "We don't have openings now."

"When will you?"

"Not for a long time. We only hiring students now, no full-time janitors."

"Well, what else do you have?"

He grabbed a stack of papers and started paging through them, reading position titles.

When he got to Computer Programmer Trainee I asked, "What do I need for that?"

"We have a test," he said. "Would you like to take it?"

"Sure, why not?"

I quickly took the test and did well.

"The Data Processing department is doing the hiring," Mr. Bachus said. "Someone will call you for an interview."

I left the office excited and asked a friend to pray for "open or closed doors."

The doors started swinging open. I got an interview. My interviewer was a basketball fan. He knew about a kid from Hudsonville who was Michigan's best high school basketball player that year. We hardly talked about the job, but we talked a lot of basketball. I left the office with his hearty best wishes.

The doors were swinging wide open and I was getting scared. I had applied for the job on a whim, but now I was getting cold feet. What if I got hired? "I know I asked for open or closed doors," I argued with God, "but I've changed my mind. I don't want white-collar work—I'm a blue-collar guy. I want to be a janitor."

Certain that a job offer was coming, I composed a "thanks, but no thanks," speech in my head. Then Diana got a call to substitute teach one morning. She left and Jeremy asked for a nap—something he never did. Suddenly, desperately tired myself, I lay down and fell into a deep sleep. The phone began ringing incessantly. I crawled back to semi-consciousness, grabbed the phone, and croaked, "Hello."

"Hi, this is Mr. Bachus from MSU. You have the job."

He went on to tell me where and when I needed to go for pre-employment physicals and such. I was still more asleep than not. I couldn't remember the speech I had planned.

Mr. Bachus finished his directions and asked, "Okay?"

"Okay, goodbye," I croaked and hung up. I turned my head upward and prayed. "Okay, Lord. You win. I'll take the job.

Glen and Diana with Jeremy, on the front steps of the Willow Street house.

Dear Grandkids,

God knew more about my needs than I did. The economy soon changed to an extended time of stagnant wages combined with inflation. The cost of everything rose quickly. I had grown accustomed to buying everything we needed while still saving a quarter of my pay. I thought that would last forever.

The new job offered better pay, better benefits, and much better career opportunities. Also, somewhat to my surprise, I had a knack for the work and enjoyed it immensely.

Love, Grandpa Glen

Diana, Jeremy, and Glen on the lawn outside MSU's Alumni Chapel.

Chapter 21 – Early Career Years

I worked in the MSU Data Processing Department for five years. The university's main computer occupied a large room with special air-conditioning to cool the equipment. This massive computer had less processing power than the phone I carry in my pocket today.

The computer read punch cards and used magnetic tapes to store data. Our son, Jeremy, was one and a half years old when I started and close to seven when I moved on. He knew that I went to work to make money. He took that quite literally, thinking I cranked it out on some machine.

Our landlord decided to sell our house and gave us the first chance to buy it. I doubted we could afford it. Something smaller and cheaper would be better. We looked at other houses on the market—lots of them, all over the area. They all cost as much or more than our own house.

I asked the couple in the other apartment to purchase it. They said they couldn't. They had just bought a new car and didn't need another payment. We had no choice. We couldn't afford a move and couldn't afford raised rents if somebody else bought our house. We signed papers and became both owners and landlords.

We took a trip to Isle Royale National Park in the summer of 1974 when Jeremy was almost three years old. Shortly before leaving, I was shopping for fishing tackle. A fellow shopper struck up a conversation, and we discovered that he and his family would be going to the island about the same time as us. He was a local lawyer with a gift for gab. His name, improbably but quite appropriately, was Wiley as in "Wile E. Coyote."

"Maybe we can fish together," Wiley proposed.

"Maybe," I offered cautiously. We exchanged information about where we would stay on the island. I didn't expect anything to come of it.

We went to Isle Royale and had a great time. We canoed from the ferry-boat landing at Rock Harbor to Moskey Basin campground and stayed all week. I portaged my roomy, lightweight, homemade canoe to Lake Richie—a two-mile trail walk. It helped that Jeremy could cover the distance on his own if we took frequent stops.

We hid the canoe near the lake, leaving it to hike back and forth from our campsite daily. Our camp meals always included delicious Northern Pike fillets fried to perfection over hot coals. We gladly shared our bounty with neighboring campers. They shared their extras as well. Jeremy especially enjoyed "Owl Pudding," butterscotch pudding in a box with the "Red Owl" logo.

The Owl Pudding camper was a young single man, a backpacker from Missouri. One evening we were sitting by the campfire talking. The topic somehow turned to maple syrup.

"I love maple syrup," he said. "We made it in Boy Scouts when I was a kid."

"Really?" I asked, "How do you make it in Missouri?"

"Easy. You buy a jar of Mapleine, add sugar and water, and cook it a few minutes."

I shook my head sadly and disabused his notion. "No, no, no! Real maple syrup comes from tapping trees and boiling sap. You'd love the real thing if you like the fake stuff."

Our delightful time at Moskey Basin came to an end, and I portaged the canoe out one evening. The next morning, we loaded our gear in the boat and prepared to shove off. It would take all day to paddle ten miles back to Rock Harbor. Just then, Wiley and his boys showed up. Their little aluminum fishing boat with a tiny outboard motor came to a stop. Wiley started to talk.

"Hey, let's go fishing."

"Sorry, I'm packed. We're leaving."

"No problem. Don't canoe back. I'll tow you later. Let's fish first."

Wiley kept talking and I finally gave in. He had a way with words. We unpacked my canoe, I hoisted it to my shoulders, and we began another portage to Lake Richie. Wiley and his boys carried the fishing gear. Diana stayed with Jeremy and our things back at camp. She was not pleased.

I reached the lake and put the canoe in the water. I sat in back, steering, while Wiley sat in front, paddling and watching for obstacles. His two young boys sat in the middle and quarreled. Bang! We hit a rock that Wiley didn't see because he was untangling his squabbling sons.

"Don't move," I shouted. "Stay where you are and I'll back off."

"I'll help," said Wiley as he stepped toward me.

It didn't help. A resounding crack split the air as Wiley straddled the rock and cracked my beautiful canoe. He's lucky I didn't smash his head with my paddle. I sure felt like it. The crack barely leaked. I could fix it after I got home, but I was mad at him and his naughty boys. I was even madder at myself for letting him talk me into this foolish expedition.

I calmed down and started to enjoy my role as fishing guide. Paddling along Lake Richie's shoreline, I pulled into the edge of a weedy cove. "Cast towards shore," I told the boys. "Let it settle a second, reel a little, make your spinner look like a frog swimming."

The boys listened, did what I said, and one soon had a fish on his line. "Keep the tip of your pole high," I continued. "Reel slowly and steadily. Bring your fish next to the boat. I'll net it."

Again, he did what I said. The boys, totally captivated now, weren't arguing anymore. I scooped the fish up, wet my hands, grabbed it behind the gills, and used an extractor to remove the hook. I slipped the fish back into the water and watched it swim away. "Why did you do that?" howled the successful fisherman with dismay. "That's the biggest fish I ever caught."

"Don't worry," I said. "You'll catch bigger ones. Little pike are skin and bones. This one was only nineteen inches. We want ones with more meat."

He looked dubious, but he and his brother kept fishing. They were both successful. With a stringer full of keepers, we were a happy group as we hiked back to camp.

"Ride in our boat with us," Wiley proposed after we loaded our canoe. "We'll tow yours."

"Are you sure that's a good idea?" I asked. "Your boat doesn't look big enough."

"It'll be fine. Don't worry. We have lots of room."

We jumped in. The boat sat low in the water as we putted down the long bay. It was smooth as glass, protected from Lake Superior's waves by a long peninsula. The rest of the way to Rock Harbor, after the peninsula, would stay protected by a series of off-shore islands. Small breaks between islands might let a few waves through, but we should have smooth sailing most of the way.

Then we came to the first break. A wave bashed the side of the boat and poured right in, almost swamping us. We bailed furiously and turned desperately toward shore. There, wet and cold, my family got out to walk the rest of the way on the shoreline trail. It was with some apprehension that we watched Wiley and the boys pull away, still towing our canoe and belongings.

We figured it would take two or three hours to reach Rock Harbor. It might be dark when we got there. Jeremy didn't want to walk anymore and was too slow anyway—he had to be carried. We took turns and trudged on. About halfway back we saw Wiley returning with an empty boat. His boys and our canoe were safely waiting at Rock Harbor. He pulled up and offered a ride, which we gratefully accepted.

We met Wiley's wife at Rock Harbor. She was gracious, patient and kind. She insisted on treating us to supper at the restaurant. She also invited us to share their motel room, complete with hot showers and warm beds. That sounded nice right then, better than camping. We enjoyed our stay and departed as friends.

Two years later, friends from church invited us to spend a week's vacation camping with them at Cran Hill Ranch. Cran Hill is a Reformed Church youth camp near Big Rapids, Michigan. It also has a campground where families can stay.

Four families from our church had gone there the previous year. They had a great time and thought we might like to join them. Diana was enthusiastic. I was hesitant. I wanted someplace with pike fishing—maybe Isle Royale. It wasn't a practical idea with our daughter, Sara, still a toddler. Reluctantly, half-heartedly, I agreed to a week at Cran Hill.

We had a fantastic time swimming, horseback riding, and visiting. Kids caught frogs by the lake. Each evening, after a potluck dinner, we lingered around the campfire—singing and sharing stories. We prayed long and well.

One evening, another dad in our group, a guy named Bruce, invited me to fish with him the next morning. He had been having good luck with bluegills. We got up early and paddled across the lake to a spot near a cove. Bluegills were biting like crazy and we started hauling them in.

Then I noticed something peculiar. I caught bluegills everywhere except for one spot where I got no action at all. I wondered if a bigger fish, a predator, lingered there. I changed my bluegill bait for a pike lure and cast it out. Immediately the pole bent, my line ran, and I knew I had hooked a big fish. When Bruce scooped it into his net, I stared at a thirty-seven-inch, twelve-pound Northern Pike. Wow! And I thought Cran Hill lacked pike fishing.

Cran Hill became a big part of our lives for almost twenty years. Our kids attended the youth camps, and Jeremy served as a counselor after high school. Our family camp grew as dozens of church families spent annual vacations at Cran Hill. Kids ran in unsupervised packs, stopping for snacks or games at various campsites. We rode a bus into town and took tubing trips down the Muskegon River. Adults shared coffee and visiting. These intense times built deep and lasting friendships.

Ironically, I almost never fished again—neither at Cran Hill nor elsewhere. I had already caught the fish of a lifetime. How could I top that?

Jeremy holding the big pike at Cran Hill Ranch. Note my homemade canoe in the background.

Dear Grandkids,

I've carved cedar fans most of my life and always dreamed of making it a career. I've sold some fans but never enough to make a living. Compared to Vincent Van Gogh, I've done alright. He completed more than nine hundred paintings during his lifetime, but sold only one. His work gained value only after his death.

In his classic work, Whittling and Woodcarving, *E. J. Tangerman describes wooden fan carving as a whittling trick. He groups it with other tricks like carving a chain from a solid stick. Not art, just a trick.*

I prefer to see it as a technique, something that can be elevated to art with the right perspective and effort. Art buyers disagree. You will inherit my best pieces. Their market value will still be little to nothing. I won't be Van Gogh.

Love, Grandpa Glen

A weathered fencepost fan, all one piece of wood.

Chapter 22 – Cedar Fan Carving

Shortly after our first time camping at Cran Hill, I met a couple of professors from MSU. This husband and wife team, C. Kurt Dewhurst and Marsha MacDowell, were launching a Michigan folk art project. My dad read about their work in a newspaper and called to ask about cedar fans. They had never heard of this craft. My dad encouraged me to contact them.

Kurt and Marsha's office in the MSU museum was a short walk from where I worked. I visited them on a lunch break, bringing some fans along. They were enthralled. My work and my dad's became a part of their 1978 *Rainbows in the Sky* book and exhibit.

About that time, my car had brake problems and a friend from church offered assistance. I'm not very mechanical but he was, so we worked together and did the job. When I offered payment, he refused saying, "I'm just glad to help."

I took a fan off my living room wall and gave it to him. He accepted that payment with, "Thanks, I've always loved John Smedley's fans."

"Who's John Smedley?"

"My neighbor from Torch Lake, a fan carver."

I made a trip to see John Smedley, dropping in unannounced. He, like my dad, had learned fan carving from his lumberjack father. He was older than my dad and said he didn't carve anymore. His health and eyesight weren't up to it. He seemed beaten down and hopeless but perked up as we talked carving. Kurt and

145

Marsha were interested in his work, too, and John soon started carving again. His health improved as he found a new passion in life. He demonstrated and sold fans all over Michigan.

My work, like John's, was enriched by Kurt and Marsha's interest and exposure. I demonstrated fan carving at a folk festival held at the Indiana Dunes National Lakeshore while Sara watched a Chippewa family dance. They gave her a simple but pretty toy deer, crafted from a wood shaving.

As I carved, I listened to a unique folk band. Their hometown in northern Sweden was a steel-making city near the Arctic Circle. Their music combined Swedish, Norwegian, Finnish, and Lapp (Sami) cultures. They walked by on break to watch me work.

One musician wore a belt knife which I admired. He took it off and handed it over for a closer look. The sheath was hand-tooled leather. The wooden handle contained intricate inlays of varying woods. A sharp, strong blade topped it off. He explained that he had made it all, even the blade.

Then he pointed to my fans. "We have this kind of carving in Sweden, but not as good."

"Thanks," I said, happy for praise from such a fine craftsman.

"No," he continued. "Our wood isn't as good."

He was right about that. You can't beat Michigan's Northern White Cedar.

In the years and decades to come, I had more acclaim and exposure, all flowing directly or indirectly from my first encounter with Kurt Dewhurst and Marsha MacDowell.

The Lansing State Journal ran several long and flattering accounts of me and my carving. A local television station aired a short feature that their network picked up and ran nationwide. A popular magazine flew a photography team to Michigan for an article on my work. The Detroit Free Press sent a photographer to do another feature story. Other books and publications added to my reputation.

I especially enjoyed my time as an artist at The Smithsonian's annual folk festival in 1987. The whole family came along. The festival provided lodging and meals for participants. We stayed two weeks at a hotel in Arlington, Virginia—several blocks from the Pentagon. Meal costs for my family were our only expense. Everything else was covered, even mileage from Michigan and back.

Each weekday I carved and shared my craft with tourists. On weekends we toured the area as a family. Diana and the kids explored museums and nearby sites every morning. They joined me at lunch time so I could take a break. I always had a crowd of thirty or forty people standing around my display. Once, a man asked, "Is it hard to split the blades that thin?"

"No," I answered. "The woodgrain does most of the work. Anybody can do it."

Just then, I saw Diana and the kids coming for my lunch break. I pointed at Jeremy behind the crowd and said, "Young man, come here."

He played along, "Me?"

"Yeah, you. Come split this fan," I said as Jeremy stepped up. "Take the knife, line it up, split it down."

Jeremy sat and did as he was told, flawlessly splitting blades with speed, precision, and skill until a bystander exclaimed, "He's a plant."

"Yes," I admitted. "This is my son but splitting really is easier than it looks."

Each evening, back at the hotel after supper, participants gathered for hours. Musicians jammed. We relaxed and visited. I especially enjoyed gospel singers from Detroit, Chippewa craftspeople from the Upper Peninsula, and a fur trapper from the northern Lower Peninsula.

Our stay included the Fourth of July. That evening the hotel staff brought us to a revolving restaurant on the top floor. It was closed for renovation, but they opened it for festival participants to watch fireworks. Floor-to-ceiling windows surrounded us. We watched at least four different displays as Washington D.C. and surrounding cities simultaneously lit up the sky. It was the best show ever.

I was honored with the Michigan Heritage Award in 2000. The presenter called me a living national treasure. High praise.

Several years later, I received an unexpected phone call from Roy Underhill. He was host of "The Woodwright's Shop," a popular show on public television. Roy offered me an honorarium and expense money if I would fly out and shoot an episode for his series. I was honored again and immediately accepted his offer.

Roy and his wife hosted me at their home in Williamsburg, Virginia. I had always wanted to visit Colonial Williamsburg, a noted living-history settlement. Roy, as a former director there, gifted me with an all-day pass. I spent a pleasant day touring the town and museum while Roy had business elsewhere.

Back at Roy's home that evening, I made a simple fan. Roy was excited and called a close friend to come watch me make another one. The next day we worked on our tentative script.

The following day, a Saturday, we drove to the University of North Carolina, in Raleigh. The university's TV studio was quiet on everybody's day off, and we worked all day practicing the show. Then on Sunday we spent a very long morning actually filming the half-hour segment. The finished product looked natural and easy. Viewers have no idea how much effort was really involved.

Several years later a community art gallery in Big Rapids, Michigan, hosted an exhibit of my carvings. I showed my newest and best work including a ten-foot-wide mobile. After the Big Rapids show, I moved the mobile to Grand Rapids, Michigan, for the annual Art

Prize competition. I received many compliments but no sales.

Diana always said that my art might make me famous but it wouldn't make me rich. She sure got that right.

Dear Grandkids,

We lived in our first Lansing home for ten years, partly as renters and partly as landlords—first in the smaller apartment and then in the larger one.

We made many improvements. Painting, roofing, insulating. New carpets.

Our biggest improvement came right at the end. Let me tell about it.

> *Love, Grandpa Glen*

Our Willow Street house.

Chapter 23 – Remodeling

University Reformed Church, a campus ministry of the Reformed Church in America (RCA), was our congregation. We rented the Alumni Chapel on Michigan State's campus for Sunday Services but were outgrowing it. Our pastor, Tom Stark, preached spiritual and intellectual sermons that attracted professors' families and students.

We needed a place of our own so the RCA helped us with funds. We bought property on Hagadorn Road across the street from campus. Two old houses stood there. One would be removed to make room for the new building. Church members were free to salvage stuff before wreckers finished the job. I pried up beautiful red oak flooring—hundreds of square feet—and hauled it home.

I wanted to replace our kitchen's bumpy old linoleum floor. A friend, Steve, came over to help on a Saturday early in 1979. Diana and the kids drove across town to spend time with Steve's family.

"Here's the plan," I explained. "We'll tear up linoleum and put down oak. We should get that done today. I'll sand and varnish the oak another day."

"Sounds good. Let's do it."

The linoleum came up easily. We opened a window behind the kitchen and pitched debris onto a growing pile in the backyard. Tongue-and-groove pine flooring appeared. It was terrible, half rotten and useless.

"This has to go," I told Steve. "I planned to lay oak over it but we'll use the sub-floor instead."

The old pine flooring joined the backyard pile. Then I stepped on the subflooring and almost fell through. It was worse than the pine. We tore it up and threw it out. Now the floor joists were fully exposed. An oak beam ran down the middle. It was strong and high but smaller joists sagged away from it. We ripped it all out. We had worked all day and were in worse shape than when we started.

When our families came to see our progress, Steve's wife Victoria exclaimed in horror, "You can't stay here! Get clothes and come to our house."

We agreed. A trip from bedrooms to bathroom would require two ladder climbs—one down to the basement and another back up. Not very practical. We gathered our stuff and went with them. The overnight stay turned into a month of living together. Fortunately, although we had been good friends before, our unplanned stay brought us even closer. Maybe it helped that I was barely there.

At that time, I was employed by the State of Michigan in downtown Lansing. Each morning I packed two sack lunches—one for noon and one for supper. I worked on our house for three or four hours every weekday and all-day Saturdays.

The MSU Spartan basketball team, led by hometown star Ervin "Magic" Johnson, was making a run that would bring them a national championship. Diana and our host family watched every exciting game on television. I missed them all.

Since I already had a big project, I decided to make it even bigger. I took down all the cupboards and fixtures. I could improve the layout of the kitchen while I was at it. Rebuilding began to take shape. Straight and level floor joists spanned the whole room. New plywood provided a solid sub-floor. I hammered the oak flooring in place and rented a sander to smooth it.

I stained and varnished the oak. Now I had a big empty room with a spectacular floor. My old kitchen-dining area had been awkward and inefficient. This was my chance for something completely different, a chance I would have missed if my original plans had worked.

I rebuilt the space, keeping doorways and walk areas on one side. The other side became an efficient kitchen and charming dining area. Delighted with improvements, we moved back home.

I still had work to do. Our kitchen had ugly painted wainscoting. I wanted something pretty. I bought red-oak plywood and cut leftover flooring for trim. I put up plywood wainscoting, trimmed with thin oak boards, and stained it to match the floor. Once more, it was lovely.

Partway through this project, we had an incident. My old wainscoting had been removed but only part of the new put up. We had a hole in one wall and a bat found a way in. We came home to find it hanging on Sara's bedroom wall.

I'm afraid of bats because I'm afraid they carry rabies. I stifled my fear and captured the bat by clapping a quart canning jar over it. Then I slipped a lid on the jar and poked air holes in the lid. I had recently read a newspaper article about an MSU professor who wanted to see rare bats. We decided to take it to him.

I found his name in the phone book, gave him a call, and drove to his home in East Lansing. Diana and the kids came along for the adventure. The professor, at work in his yard, looked the part. He had longish white hair and long moustaches. He glanced at our glass jar and quickly proclaimed that this was a common brown bat, not the rare kind he wanted.

Then he reached in, deftly removing the bat with his bare hand. He held it by both wings and spread them wide. I stared in amazement and asked, "Don't bats carry rabies?"

"Sometimes," he casually replied. "But sometimes dogs and people do too."

I was dubious. Bats carry rabies more than dogs and people. I wasn't a professor but I knew that much. Maybe he had been vaccinated, like veterinarians do to pets.

The professor loved his rapt audience. He explained bat anatomy to Jeremy and Sara. He showed the correspondence between the bat's wing bones and our own hand bones. All the while, the bat was protesting. It squeaked and struggled, turning its head as it tried to bite the professor. It missed but nipped its own wing. Bright red blood appeared.

The professor said, "Don't hurt yourself sweetheart," as he casually wiped the blood on his blue jeans. The bat grabbed his jeans with sharp little teeth and claws. It held on until the professor gently pried it loose. He flung it into the air where it caught wing and flew swiftly away.

Sara asked in a concerned voice, "What will happen to it?"

"Bats have great homing instincts," the professor happily answered. "It will probably be back in your house before you are."

I quickly thanked him, hurried home, and instantly covered any possible bat opening. We never had another one.

Meanwhile, Lansing Christian School had purchased an old public-school building. The Christian School's elementary grades would move there the next school year. Jeremy was a Lansing Christian student. We were pleased that the school helped us raise children of faith. Sara would also attend but hadn't started school yet.

We went to the open house for the new school late that summer. I dropped the family off and parked around the block. Our walk back took a shortcut through the playground. A charming two-story brick home with a for-sale sign sat by our car. I joked, "You wouldn't have to drive kids to school if we lived here."

"Let's look at it," said Diana.

"No, we just finished remodeling and can't afford it anyway."

"Let's look. It's probably ugly inside. We won't even like it when we see it."

We agreed to look and admired its high ceilings, nice fireplace, warm oak trim, and big rooms. We loved the house and eventually made an offer. It was accepted and our old home was on the market. It took a while to sell but we made a handsome profit. Our remodeling had paid off.

The new place would be our home until both kids were grown and married. Many great memories were built there. The kids loved to share our pool—a large, round, above-ground model—with neighborhood friends. Walking to school was convenient, especially in later years when Diana taught there. It was a good move.

Our Sparrow Street house.

Dear Grandkids,

The early 1980s was a busy time as we raised children. Both kids were at Lansing Christian School. Tuition wasn't cheap, but we never regretted our decision to send them there.

Your grandmother was a stay-at-home mom despite being a fully-qualified teacher. Sometimes she worked part-time but never at anything that kept her away when kids were home. We never regretted that decision either.

Our decisions were right for our family, but it was a struggle financially.

Those were wise priorities for us then. May you be blessed with wise priorities all your lives.

Love Grandpa Glen

Glen and Diana, Jeremy and Sara, on the "Looking for a Shell Station" vacation.

Chapter 24 – Early Eighties

We planned a camping trip for the summer of 1982. It would take us through New York and New England, up the coast of Maine, and back home through Quebec and Ontario. We were a little low on funds but thought we could cover expenses by selling cedar fans.

I carved a batch and was accepted to an art show. Then I had a bad infection that kept me from doing the show. My nice fans remained unsold and our trip money evaporated. We had a gasoline card for Shell stations but no other credit cards. If we bought all our gas from Shell and were careful with other spending, we could take the trip.

Our plan worked flawlessly until we hit New York State. The first town had no Shell station. It became a pattern repeated in every town after that. We always found former Shell stations that had closed or switched to another company. We never found any that honored our credit card. We dipped into cash and became ever more careful with other expenses.

In Vermont, we had a wonderful time visiting with our friends Steve and Kathy. Their son and daughter were close in age to our kids. We drove on and camped at Acadia National Park in Maine, still never finding a Shell station. Finally, someone told us, "Shell pulled out of New York and New England a year ago."

At one campground, we became friends with a young couple camped nearby. I wondered about their southern accent and asked, "Where are you from?"

I was surprised when the young lady answered, "Massachusetts."

It didn't sound like a Massachusetts accent to me. I probed deeper, "Anyplace before that?"

"Nashville, Tennessee."

"What brought you to Massachusetts?"

"I'm a student at Gordon-Conwell Theological Seminary," her husband answered. "We live near Boston."

Meanwhile, Sara amused herself climbing my back and sitting on my shoulders. I flipped her down and she climbed again. I carried on my conversation as if Sara wasn't there. The young wife was surprised and aghast. She stared at Sara and asked, "Y'all think your daddy's a tree?"

We talked about marriage. They had dated all through high school and college. They thought they knew each other well and were surprised when marriage wasn't an easy adjustment. "I never want to go through that first year again," the husband said. 'We didn't even use toothpaste in the same way. Things are going fine now, but the first year was hard."

We passed many roadside stands offering fresh-cooked lobster, and the kids kept begging to try some. I kept putting them off. Diana asked, "Why don't you stop?"

"Anticipation," I answered, "is the best part".

Eventually we did stop at a stand and bought two lobsters. Both Jeremy and Sara took one bite and declared they were done. The unfamiliar taste was not to their liking. Diana and I enjoyed a most delightful dinner while the kids feasted on Campbell's Chunky Soup.

After Acadia, on our way home through Quebec, we found Shell stations again. We were so happy that we celebrated with a meal at McDonalds. The next day, when we came to a toll station on the expressway, I asked about the exchange rate. I had been treated fairly at McDonalds and expected the same here.

The steely-eyed government official coldly informed me, "We aren't a bank here."

"What rate can you give me?"

"Flat up, dollar for dollar."

I had been getting $1.30 Canadian for an American dollar. I shrugged and handed him my smallest bill, a ten. He ostentatiously opened his own wallet and exchanged my money for a Canadian ten. His bill went in the till and my Canadian change came from it. The thirty percent difference stayed in his wallet.

We quickly drove out of Quebec and camped that night in Ontario. At a campground that evening, I stood in line to pay my fee. Another camper with New York plates and a New York accent held out an American ten-dollar bill. In an accusing and belligerent tone he asked, "How much will you rip me off?"

"Rip you off?"

"Yeah, how much will you charge to take American money."

"No charge, we give $1.30 Canadian for every dollar American."

"That's as good as a bank!"

"Of course."

We drove on the next day and reached the Windsor tunnel across from Detroit. We pulled into line and counted our money. Toll for the tunnel was $1.50. We didn't have it. Our kids dug into their leftover spending money. All four of us were able to pool $1.50 (with a few cent's left over) to buy our way back to the USA.

We were driving an ancient station wagon in the mid-80s. The original red paint had oxidized and the finish was now covered with a thin white film. Sara was interested in past presidents and used our car as a whiteboard, scratching president's names and terms of office all over the car. We had no idea that she would one day marry a member of the Harrison family. Two presidents from that family were scrawled on our car when Sara was a 10-year-old.

We took that car to a friend's wedding in Oakland County. When we drove up to the posh country club door, a valet took our keys and parked the car. We enjoyed a very nice wedding and long reception. Eventually, we said our goodbyes and stepped out. A valet walked up and asked, "Your car, sir?"

"It's an old station wagon…"

"The Malibu sir. One moment sir."

If I had answered, "I have a Mercedes" or "I'm driving a BMW," he would have asked, "Your license plate, sir?"

We took another trip with the Malibu. It ran great, easily climbing Colorado's highest passes while pulling our camping trailer. We hiked in the mountains with our friends Joe and Louise. Joe approached a high snowfield, a patch still unmelted in mid-summer. Wearing heavy hiking boots with deep treads, he ran and slid. His boots acted like skis. He went a short distance and swerved to a stop. It looked like fun.

"Let's try it dad," Sara said. "Let's hold hands and ski together."

We started slowly but our tennis shoes were slippery and we started speeding towards a steep slope. "Dig your heels in," Joe yelled. "Dig your heels in."

We tried, but it only slowed us a little. I desperately prayed, "Lord, save us."

We sped toward a boulder field below. I grabbed Sara and hugged her tight, trying to protect her. I extended my legs and tried to absorb impact from the first boulder. It was the size of a kitchen stove and many more followed it. We flew into the air and tumbled down. Coming to a stop, we picked ourselves up, bruised and shaken, but not seriously injured. We could have suffered closed-head injuries, broken bones, or even death. We were blessed to get off so easily.

Meanwhile, Sara had been begging for cat. Our old kitty had died some years before. We told her she could have a kitten for her June birthday, but not until we returned from vacation. Sara declared, "A home is just not a home without a cat."

She had a specific cat in mind. It had to be a male gray tabby. After vacation, we looked at newspaper ads, signs on telephone poles, and grocery store bulletin boards. We made phone calls. We struck out. We couldn't find Sara's cat. At last, Diana drove home from a grocery store where people sometimes stood with boxes of free kittens. She was frustrated and prayed, "Lord if you want us to have a cat, please just send one."

Diana started unloading groceries. Just then, Sara ran home from across the street, carrying a gray, tabby, male kitten. He looked lethargic, scrawny, and ragged. "This is a stray," she said. "Mr. Cook has been feeding him and said we can have him. May we please?"

Diana silently asked, "Lord, is this a joke?"

"This kitty looks awful," she said aloud. "Are you sure you want him?"

"Oh," Sara answered, "but he needs a home."

He did indeed. Sarah named him Chester after Chester Allen Arthur, the US president. Chester, the kitty, happily ate everything we fed him and perked up quickly. A day or two later he was home alone. We returned to find an empty fishbowl with half the water splashed out. Chester smelled suspiciously of goldfish. From then on, Chester got a goldfish for his birthday treat each year. We decreed that the cat and Sara shared a birthday—it had to be close.

Chester grew to become a large and loving cat, a wonderful pet, not a joke at all—a perfect answer to prayer.

Sara and Chester in our front yard.

Dear Grandkids,

My job history is full of twists and turns that eventually took us up north to live.

Let me tell you a bit about it.

> *Love, Grandpa Glen*

The Priority Health building where Glen had a
second-floor corner office overlooking
the East Beltline in Grand Rapids.

Chapter 25 – More Job History

In 1984 my friend Allan asked if I would work for him. It was a tempting offer. Allan had a PhD in systems science. He was head honcho of the Information Systems team at Blue Care Network-Health Central, Blue Cross's mid-Michigan HMO.

Allan usually hired only beginning programmers, but it wasn't working well. Now he had authorization to hire a more experienced person and offered me a position. I appreciated the opportunity but didn't want to be known as the guy who got hired as the boss's friend.

"I'll take the job," I promised, "but only if you post, advertise, and hire on qualifications alone."

"Good idea," he replied.

He ended up with two finalists—myself and a fellow named Bob. Bob decided he would rather work as an independent consultant. That left me as the obvious choice for the position. Allan took Bob on as a consultant as well, and we made a great team. Bob sped through his work but grew bored with details. I cleaned up and finished up. Between the two of us we produced quick and thorough work.

I loved working at Health Central. Allan was a great boss and a great friend. Sometimes we took a break to walk around the neighborhood and pray together.

Health Central was a mixed-model HMO with staff doctors on-site and contracted physicians around the area. Our software, purchased from a Detroit company, covered everything from insurance processing to patient appointments. It came with underlying code, an unusual feature in the software world, so we could modify it as we wished.

My department functioned like a little software company but with one key difference. We had our users under the same roof. This allowed us to get immediate feedback whenever we wrote new programs. I loved this aspect of my work and wondered how big companies functioned without it.

Allan eventually left the company and struck out on his own as a consultant. Doug, a retired Army officer with a Master's Degree, was hired in his place. We worked well together. I managed programming staff while he managed the rest of the department and attended meetings with superiors.

Sometime later, the company ran into a budget shortfall and decided to cut staff. My boss, Doug, was dismissed. I was immediately informed that I had been promoted to his position. I would do my job and his. I had enjoyed working with Allan and Doug but liked this role even more. I delighted in hiring the best possible people and found satisfaction in encouraging and developing their talents.

One of my most satisfying experiences came from serving on a small task force that reviewed positions for hundreds of employees. We used the Hay Group methodology, the premier method in the business. I loved the logic and order behind the system.

I developed a way to prioritize work requests, replacing a constant scramble to accommodate everyone immediately. We developed lists for small, medium, and large tasks. A different person handled small requests each week. Medium and large requests were addressed at regular meetings with key users. We reached consensus and worked accordingly. I was happy that my staff now used their time more wisely.

Blue Cross owned several HMOs, each with its own software system. Transitioning to a single system became top priority for my staff and me. We worked on it for two years, did it well, and were honored by our corporate board for a job well done.

I led a capable group of college graduates, and decided that I should have more schooling too. I applied to a new program at MSU, pursuing a Master's Degree in Non-Profit Management.

My application proposed that undergraduate education consists of two parts—two years of liberal-arts and two years of job training. I argued that I had fulfilled them both, the first at MSU and the second on the job. I added letters of recommendation to back up my claim.

My Graduate Record Exam results were pretty good, except for the math portion. I hadn't taken math since high school and neglected to study up. My math percentile was only 56—not good enough. I didn't get into the program.

Shortly after that, I received an amazing opportunity. Health Central's second in command was hired to run the Mayo Clinic HMOs. She would be moving to Minnesota and offered to take me along. It was a breathtaking offer, one that no other Health Central employee received.

Diana and I talked it over and prayed about it. On the one hand, it was a once-in-a-lifetime career move with great pay. On the other hand, we would disrupt our family at a key time when our kids were finishing high school. We decided to stay put, and I sadly declined the offer.

Eventually, I switched employers anyway. My job at Health Central was changing, and I expected my role to shrink or disappear. Several friends from work had taken jobs with Priority Health, an HMO in Grand Rapids, Michigan. I soon interviewed and was hired for a management position. I joined a daily carpool with former Health Central employees.

One perk of working at Priority was running during each lunch hour with my new friend, Steve. He was a former college runner and fifteen years my junior. I ran the best I had in years but pushed too hard, encountered injuries, and had to back off.

After a while my carpool dissolved as the others moved to Grand Rapids. With both kids out of the house, I decided that we would also make the move or find other employment. I found a new job position in Lansing, and was pondering whether to take it or move to GR.

Then I saw a newspaper ad for a job in Cadillac. It would be a demotion in pay and responsibility, but would allow us to move to our Tustin property.

I interviewed for the job and was accepted. We had a trilemma, three jobs to choose from. We chose Cadillac. It was a career-limiting move, but it took us north to where we meant to end up some day.

Our Tustin Property

Dear Grandkids,

We have lived right where we do now for all of your lives. You will always remember this house as Grandpa and Grandma's house. This next chapter will include the story of how this house came to be.

It's a house that works well for us, especially when you all come to visit. It's not the house we were planning when we moved north, but we're glad to have it.

You like it too, don't you?

Love, Grandpa Glen

Our new home under construction.

Chapter 26 – New Jobs, New Home

I started my new job at the Cadillac hospital at the end of June in 1997—arranging for two weeks of unpaid leave in July. A friend at work nicknamed me "Part-timer."

We were going west to see Rob and Sara in Vancouver, British Columbia. We packed our station wagon floor to ceiling with things to take, even filling my dad's old cartop carrier. It barely left room to sit. We had our luggage, their wedding presents, and everything Sara wanted from her bedroom. Our old car was sluggish and heavy.

The car handled funny so I volunteered for all the driving. The Montana portion of our trip—almost eight hundred expressway miles—had no speed limits then. I held a steady seventy-five miles per hour, but Diana was nervous. She kept telling me to slow down.

Sara and her husband, Rob, were just moving to a new place. We spent our first night in Vancouver at Rob's old apartment while they slept in their new rental unit across town. We helped them move the rest of their stuff the next day.

Meanwhile, our home in Lansing was listed with a realtor. We got a good offer and sealed the deal with faxes back and forth between British Columbia and Michigan. On our way home we stopped to visit a tiny mountain town in Washington State that had been used as a set for the "Northern Exposure" television show about a fictional Alaskan village. We loved the show and loved walking around town.

Diana hadn't driven on the way out, but now that the car was empty, she drove much of the way home. She sped across Montana at eighty miles per hour and more. She wasn't nervous when she was behind the wheel.

Back home, Diana got busy packing and sorting as we prepared to move. She held a yard sale and culled our belongings. I stayed north each week for work and traveled home on weekends. On Labor Day weekend, a moving company brought our stuff north. We drove our own car with our cat, Chester, in a carrier. He hated the trip, howling and yowling the whole three hours.

Uncle Alan and Aunt Leah graciously let us move into their old farmhouse rent-free. It had plumbing and heating, unlike our own little house. Their property also held a large pole barn and their own new home. I was once again their closest neighbor, just like when I was a baby. Chester loved the farmhouse, especially catching baby red squirrels in the woodshed.

Our plans were set. We would stay at Alan and Leah's all winter, purchase a modular home in the spring, and move into it a month or two later. Our house would be a manufactured Cape Cod set on an unfinished basement. We would also leave the upstairs unfinished for a while. I intended to work five years before retiring to life as a full-time cedar-fan carver.

We contacted a local builder and asked him to pour our foundation and set our new home. He listened to our plans and proposed another solution. "I can build a better home for the same money," he said. "It will be built from scratch and better quality."

When he came back with a plan, it wasn't quite what we wanted, so I drew my own plan—to scale—on graph paper. Diana looked at my plan and offered several improvements. I drew again. I visualize well but Diana needs something more concrete. We made scale-sized furniture cutouts and arranged them in various ways.

We kept improving the plans, but our progress was agonizingly slow. This led to a heated discussion as we drove home from Grand Rapids one day. I grew frustrated and angry. "You only tell me what you don't want," I blurted. "Why don't you tell me what you do want?"

"I don't know what I want," she sobbed.

We drove on in stony silence. At home, I picked up our mail and found a letter from friends in Lansing. They were participating in Engage Encounter, a Christian ministry that helps couples prepare for marriage. One exercise required writing a letter to a couple whose marriage they admired. They wrote a sweet and charming note to us, highlighting the tenderness between us.

I choked up as I read the letter aloud, gave Diana a hug, and promised to be more patient. We kept refining our plans until we both loved them. Then, a local business created blueprints. We hired a friend from church as our builder and started the project. We were fascinated that summer as paper plans became a real house.

Meanwhile, Diana missed teaching. She had taught full-time for several years at Lansing Christian Elementary School. It offered low pay but the work was rewarding. She missed the classroom and the kids. Now she talked to random kids in grocery stores. It was time to get back to school.

Diana contacted our local Pine River District and the nearby Cadillac Public Schools, adding her name as an available substitute teacher in both. A week or two later she got a call and taught a day. After a slow start, the calls picked up. The schools saw that she was available and did a good job. She soon worked daily in one district or another. She once worked every day for six weeks without repeating a classroom.

By the end of the year, her services were in demand for the next year. Diana was offered a long-term sub position for fall semester in Pine River. She would be covering for a teacher on maternity leave. The following semester she had a similar job in Cadillac. Both districts wanted to hire her full-time for the following year.

She chose our local Pine River District. We had lost half our income by moving north, partly from my voluntary demotion and the rest from Diana quitting her job. Now we made it all back. The difference in salaries between private and public schools covered the gap. We hadn't expected this blessing when we moved.

Diana continued teaching full-time for 10 years. At one time or another, she taught in each of Pine River's three elementary buildings. Many of her students claimed she was their best teacher ever. She loved her students and worked conscientiously.

My job was more frustrating. I was no longer in charge of anyone but myself. It pained me to see poor people promoted and good people ignored—such a waste of talent. I kept to my desk and did my own job well, but I missed the challenge of more responsibility. I was glad when I eventually retired.

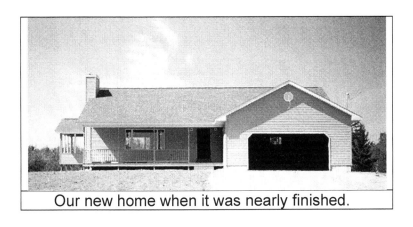
Our new home when it was nearly finished.

Dear Grandkids,

I started hiking the North Country Trail several years ago with my friend, Steve. We've covered a lot of miles since then. It has been a great adventure. I hope you enjoy the outdoors as much as I do.

Love, Grandpa Glen

Glen and Steve on the North Country Trail.

Chapter 27 – Hiking

A lady who was new to the Cadillac area started attending our church in the fall of 2013. I asked what brought her here.

She replied, "My husband, Steve, recently retired after a career working with tribal health organizations around the U.S. We lived in Minnesota, Montana, Alaska, and New Mexico, but he wanted to retire to Northern Michigan."

"Why here?" I wondered.

"He wanted someplace not far from relatives in Ohio," she answered. "He's a good swimmer and wanted a town with a year-round pool. He also wanted someplace with cross-country ski trails. Cadillac met all the criteria."

Steve sounded like my kind of guy. I quickly made arrangements to ski with him as winter fell. We enjoyed skiing together at least once a week. Spring came, snow melted, and skiing was done. Steve proposed, "Let's hike to keep in shape for skiing. I heard there's a trail that crosses Michigan. We should try it."

I agreed and Googled "trail across Michigan." Up popped the Michigan Shore-to-Shore Trail in the northern part of the Lower Peninsula. It allows hiking, but it's mainly used for horseback riding. I set aside the Shore-to-Shore and looked again.

Aha! I found the North Country Trail, a National Scenic Trail maintained by the National Park Service—a sister trail to the much more famous Appalachian Trail.

Starting at New York's border with Vermont, the NCT crosses seven states before ending in the middle of North Dakota. Its total length is over 4,500 miles including almost 1,200 miles in Michigan. Michigan's portion starts south of Jackson on the Ohio border, snakes through both peninsulas, and ends near Lake Superior at the Wisconsin border.

I had never heard of the North Country Trail. I was surprised to see that a national trail passes within thirty miles of my house. Yet, it was actually that close at several points—to the west, north, and northwest. We decided to try it.

We drove two cars to the Udall Trailhead and left one there. We drove the other vehicle south to the Freesoil Trailhead and hiked back north. After the hike, we retrieved the other car. We loved the trail. We ordered maps, planned more hikes, and kept hiking once or twice a week all through the summer in 2014. We always took two cars and hiked north, traveling light and fast from trailhead to trailhead.

Eventually, we came to an area where the North Country Trail shared a section with the Michigan-Shore-to-Shore Trail, merging, dividing, and rejoining. We didn't always know which trail we were following. The Shore-to-Shore portions were heavily eroded from horse traffic, and we trudged through deep sand. It was rough going on a hot day, so we walked with heads down, watched our steps, and missed a turn when the NCT veered off.

We kept going for several miles, somewhat puzzled by the lack of blue blazes, the usual guide marks on the

NCT. We were still seeing guide marks—the Shore-to-Shore ones—and figured the trails were still merged.

Finally, we suspected we were on the wrong trail. I checked my map and compass and found that we were way off. We revised our plan, headed cross-country to a road, and found the NCT again. We were too exhausted to double back and hike the miles we missed that day, but we returned later and hiked the right trail. We learned to watch more carefully for blue blazes and to double back quickly if we lost them.

Meanwhile, we read blogs and books and learned hiker lore and language—like the difference between day-hikers, section-hikers, and through-hikers. Day hikers like us hold the lowest status in the hiker community as we casually stroll our short walks. Section hikers, covering hundreds of miles per trip, are taken more seriously. Through hikers, the most serious of the bunch, hike thousands of miles in a season to cover a long trail from end to end.

Once, as we sat in the shade and ate lunch, a young woman stopped to talk. She asked if we were hikers. "Yes, I answered, "but just day-hikers."

"That's good," she said. "I'd hate to hike in the dark."

Apparently, she didn't know hiker terms and lore.

That fall, we met the Grand Traverse Hiking Club challenge by completing their 101-mile portion of the North Country Trail. Now we felt like real hikers.

Ski season came again. We began to see cross-country skiing as conditioning for hiking, instead of the other way around. We kept hiking north in 2015 and reached the Mackinaw Bridge by Labor Day. There, we joined tens of thousands for the annual Labor Day Bridge Walk. It's the only time that this part of the NCT can be traversed on foot.

Hiking weather lasted into November that year. We turned our attention to the southbound trail, starting again at the Freesoil Trailhead. One late October day, on a trail deep in the woods, we saw a young couple with backpacks and trekking poles hiking quickly toward us. They stopped to talk, and we learned that they had through-hiked the lengthy, strenuous Pacific Crest Trail a year earlier. It was an honor to spend fifteen or twenty minutes with them; it felt like meeting royalty.

Our winter flew by, and the 2016 hiking season brought a new goal: completing the rest of the southbound trail to the Ohio border. An early start to our hiking season, combined with increased distances for each hike, soon made the distance between home and trail too daunting for one-day trips. We began driving to campgrounds, sleeping in tents each night, and hiking several days in a row. We enjoyed the camping—two retired guys reliving their youth.

One evening, at a little restaurant in a southern Michigan town, another diner approached and asked if we were hikers. She had noticed Steve's T-shirt with its NCT map on the back. We admitted we were, and she said that she was a hiker too. She was a teacher, section-hiking the Appalachian Trail, biting off a new portion each summer.

The last hike to the Ohio border was mostly a walk along open roadside—instead of shaded trails—on a stifling day as the sun beat down without mercy. Steve had trouble keeping a fast pace, but I wasn't helpful. I kept pushing the pace and checking the time. We had one more mission that day.

We wanted to reach the NCT headquarters in Lowell before closing time so we could collect 100-mile challenge awards for our two hundred miles hiked that year. Our arrival was a little late, but the gracious staff opened the door and cheerfully helped us at the end of their busy day.

Although it was fortunate that we received our awards, it was unfortunate that I'd pushed Steve too hard. He'd had past problems with atrial fibrillation and his a-fib returned during that hike. Our usual autumn hiking season didn't happen that year as Steve received treatment to restore his normal heart rhythm.

Steve felt fine as the 2017 hiking season started, so we chose a new goal: we would walk north and west from the Straits of Mackinaw and reach Marquette for the annual NCT Celebration in July. We enjoyed Michigan's Upper Peninsula but fell short of our goal.

Our last hike before the celebration was a few miles east of Grand Marais. The blue blazes led us straight to a river and stopped. We looked for a riverbank trail or a bridge but saw neither. This was new and baffling, and sunset was approaching, so we backtracked and walked a dirt road back to our car.

The NCT Association Annual Celebration in Marquette was great fun with its well-planned outings and excellent seminars. We loved being in a crowd that shared our enthusiasm for hiking. We especially enjoyed talking to Ruth and Dan Dorrough. They shared our taste for two-car day hiking, and it amazed us that they had hiked the entire North Country Trail that way, even though it took them fifteen or twenty years.

That August, after the Annual Celebration in Marquette, we took one more hiking trip. We had learned at the festival that the trail sometimes goes right through a river, so we went back to the spot that had confused us. We waded across, found blue blazes, and proceeded to hike through Grand Marais. The next day, we hiked well into the Pictured Rocks National Lakeshore and had now covered the entire eight hundred trail miles from the Ohio-Michigan border northward.

We met our hardest challenges all too soon. Steve's a-fib came back, requiring another procedure to reset his heart, and I also felt unwell. I soon learned that I had stage-four cancer, which my oncologist diagnosed as incurable and too advanced to treat with surgery.

Chemotherapy could extend my life somewhat, but my chance of living five more years was about ten percent, which meant that my chance of finishing the NCT would be slim indeed. I began an every-other-week chemotherapy regimen. These treatments beat the tumors back significantly, and I tolerated them well. I still hiked on my off weeks.

As we entered the 2018 hiking season, Steve was strong and healthy, and my cancer was somewhat at bay. We hiked when we could, picking up in the Upper Peninsula where we had left off. We wanted to finish the NCT Michigan miles and then start on other states. We were learning that hiking with a goal is different from just walking, and we were finding that aspirations are important.

Hiking in the U.P., we came across a stretch of ancient, now-forested sand dunes. Sometimes the trail had us scrambling straight up or down the steep side of a dune. Steve observed, with a wry smile, that life is often like that trail. We go up one hill and down another, sometimes striding and sometimes scrambling on all fours.

We are still striding and scrambling, savoring a love for life and love for the trail, marching on. Steve and I are day-hikers—just day-hikers—but we have learned a thing or two about trails, about hiking, and about life.

Glen on the NCT.

Dear Grandkids,

I continued to enjoy my hikes with Steve and all the scenery that we saw on the way. Through hikers only see the trail. People touring by car rarely get to remote roads.

Our style of hiking has brought us to many a scenic byway by car and many beautiful sights along the trail. We feel like we've seen the best of both worlds.

Love, Grandpa Glen

Trail maintenance
on the North Country Trail.

Chapter 28 - Pressing On

I sat with new friends in early May at the end of a great day at the 2019 NCTA Celebration, reflecting on interesting hikes, marvelous breakout sessions, and a savory supper. Now the annual awards were being announced.

Several people at my table, and many others besides, were recognized for their contributions to the North Country Trail. I applauded their efforts but also considered my own nonparticipation. I had already hiked nine hundred unique miles on the NCT and had re-walked some sections many times. Yet, I had never done a lick of trail maintenance. I quietly decided to mend my ways.

A few days later, I signed on for a workday with my local chapter, the Spirit of the Woods. This brought me to a trailhead deep in the Manistee National Forest on a sunny mid-May morning. A work trailer and a small group of workers were already there.

Our crew leader gave us safety instructions and announced that we would be working on a section of boardwalk that had been damaged by winter storms and toppled trees. It was over half a mile down the trail, and although tools could be transported by wheelbarrow, replacement lumber would be hand-carried.

I picked up four two-by-fours, each of them eight feet long, balanced them on my shoulder, and confidently strode down the trail. Wow, the load was heavier than I expected. Every board was new pressure-treated lumber that was still saturated with moisture. I paused, shifted the load to my other shoulder, and proceeded more slowly.

A wood thrush darted from the forest floor and flew to a low branch. A Sandhill Crane trumpeted its haunting call from the far side of the marsh. I continued on, shifting and pausing, again and again, until I finally made it to the worksite.

I dropped my load of lumber and checked on the repair work. Our crew was carefully prying broken boards away from wood that was still usable. Some stubborn bolts had welded themselves to their timbers and required extra effort (and ingenuity) to separate them without creating more damage.

While hiking the North Country Trail, I rarely encounter another hiker. It's rarer yet to meet a long-distance hiker, so I was delighted when a young woman with a backpack and trekking poles stopped and chatted with us. Her name was Annie and she was from Minnesota. She was a few days into a "half-through hike," an attempt to walk from central Michigan to trail's-end in North Dakota.

Annie went on her way and I continued my own trekking, making multiple trips carrying new lumber to the work site and ferrying old dry broken boards out. Each step gave me new appreciation for the dedicated volunteers who make our trail possible.

The Spirit of the Woods chapter of the North Country Trail Association is responsible for seventy-eight miles of trail plus five miles of spur trails. These distances include numerous boardwalks that total nearly a mile of six-inch-wide boards. All this building and maintenance, plus other trail work, is being done by relatively few people.

My chapter, joined by dozens of other chapters across our eight states, depends on volunteers to maintain five thousand miles of trail. I stand in awe of these volunteers and count it a privilege to join them in their efforts.

Our first NCT hiking trip of 2019 started on May 22nd at a trailhead north of Marquette, where Steve and I had ended the previous year. Our first day out was rocky and hilly but uneventful. Our second day should have been an easy walk on quiet sandy roads, but the previous week's heavy rains had melted winter's near-record snowfall. We hiked a puddled and muddy trail.

Just driving trucks to our end point was exciting as large puddles, some one-hundred-fifty-feet-long, covered the road. We saw tracks where other vehicles had crossed. Should we try? Sure, why not? We splashed in and made it through water up to our bumpers. We misunderstood a marker, drove several more bad miles, backtracked to the right turn, and finally came to the deepest and longest puddle. Should we try it? Not this time. It was a mile short of where we wanted to place a vehicle, but it would have to do.

We hiked twelve miles that second day and saw only five vehicles in all those road miles. We skirted puddles by trekking off to the side on higher ground, never needing to wade. Near the end of the day an interesting guy named Ed came to greet us. Many folks living along the trail don't even know it's there, but Ed knew the NCT and loved to talk about it.

That evening we camped beside a young woman who was bicycling around Lake Superior. Steve asked, "Why May? Why so early?"

Her reply: "It's cold or bugs. I'd rather have cold." Now, that's someone who knows the U.P!

We hiked again near the end of June, our second trip. We found all the bugs that the young woman missed in May, and then some. DEET-less repellants barely worked, and we quickly bought the real stuff.

My younger brother (Steve's age) had been doing daily walking and wanted to join us on this trip. He did well even though we had a grueling first day with steep and rugged hills. We had planned to cover seventeen miles, taking us to and through the McCormick Tract— a designated-wilderness area without blue blazes. Instead, cut off saplings and occasional rock cairns marked the trail.

We followed the trail easily, even on a posted detour marked by strips of orange tape on trees. Then we came to another place where the trail disappeared. Again, orange-taped trees led off to the side. We followed the detour for a quarter mile or so before coming to a recently logged area. It was clearly not the McCormick Tract, and we retraced our steps. We still couldn't find the trail, so we turned back to the clear-cut and trudged logging roads a while. Then, navigating by map and compass, we swerved back into the McCormick Tract.

We were barely back in the woods when Steve cried, "There's a cairn!" We were on right trail again and quickly hiked toward Steve's truck. We finished at 8:30

that evening with eighteen to twenty miles behind us. We still had to get supper and retrieve our other vehicle. It was almost midnight before we got to sleep. My brother wondered what he'd gotten into.

The second day would be easier, just eleven miles. This day's hike took us to, and almost through, Craig Lake State Park—Michigan's wildest. It treated us with a bear, the first one we'd ever seen on the trail. The lone two-year-old scrambled up a tree that leaned away from the path. There he sat fifty feet up, staring back at us. We stared too, casting cautious glances for a nearby momma bear. Fortunately, there was none to be seen. My brother was glad he'd come along.

Our planned hike for the third and last day would take us through the rest of Craig Lake State Park and then down a series of road walks. We hoped to cover thirteen new miles, but I had lost my map. I used the strong signal at Van Riper State Park to access the NCTA web site and its maps online. I copied the part I needed, more or less, on paper. It should work. What could go wrong?

I would soon find out. Our planned thirteen-mile hike turned into a twelve-mile trek that only added three new NCT miles. We missed a turn and traveled way too far on the wrong back-country two-tracks. Fortunately, this also brought us some of our best wildlife sightings. First, we saw a bull moose with velvet antlers standing some thirty yards away. Then we surprised a whole family of otters in a pond close to the road. We were almost glad for our mistake.

Our third trip took us north at the end of July. The west end of Michigan's Upper Peninsula was now an eight-hour drive from home. We paused for a quick out-and-back hike to pick up two miles missed by our previous trip's confusion. Baraga State Park, near the Keweenaw Bay Indian Community, was our chosen campground this time. A powwow was scheduled for the coming weekend and the place was crowded. US Highway 41 ran alongside the campground and contributed little to the ambiance.

Our first full hiking day was a fifteen-mile road walk, mostly on deserted dirt byways. We especially enjoyed seeing a family of trumpeter swans in a beaver flooding, even though we had to wade through an edge of that pond. Soon, we had another treat when a pair of coyotes trotted across the road in front of us. They were looking the other way and never knew we were there.

The second day was a delight. We started at Canyon Falls Roadside Park, hiked down to the falls, and through the canyon. This stretch was especially pretty, easily ranking as my second favorite after the Pictured Rocks National Lakeshore.

After three nights at Baraga State Park, we moved to the nearby Big Lake State Forest Campground. We traded narrow, noisy sites for spacious lots. We traded traffic noise for wind sighing in the pines, hot showers for a warm lake with a sandy bottom, and crowds for solitude. It was a good trade.

We spent several more wonderful days hiking before heading home. This would be our last trip of the season. We expected more trips, but things kept coming up. Good things like an Alaska cruise. Bad things like having my cancer reappear after months of clear scans.

I learned a lot that hiking season. Too late for the McCormick Tract-Craig Lake section, I learned to use more detailed maps from the NCTA website. Better yet, I learned to download a free Avenza app to my cell-phone—complete with interactive trail maps that show my exact position. It hardly uses any power on airplane mode. I kick myself for not using it earlier.

I love the North Country Trail. It brings new surprises every time I hike it, whether I'm re-hiking a familiar section or pressing on with totally new miles. I always find something special along the way. Steve and I started hiking the NCT in 2014. Our sixth season and over one thousand un-repeated miles are behind us—almost all of Michigan from Ohio to Wisconsin. We had hoped to hike the rest of Michigan's Upper Peninsula in 2019. We tried but fell short by 139 miles, leaving a goal for 2020.

We'd like to finish Michigan and tackle Wisconsin while also starting Ohio. Can it happen? Who knows? We'll try, a step at a time, enjoying each step along the way—even the detours and delays.

Dear Grandkids,

I grew up in a church that emphasized "witnessing." We were supposed to tell others about the gospel.

Sometimes, this was accomplished by handing out tracts (Christian pamphlets) in downtown Grand Rapids. I always felt awkward and embarrassed by such activities.

I could talk to almost anyone about almost anything except my faith. It's odd. I hope to grow in this area.

I hope that you, too, have a vibrant faith that you can share as you live out your days.

Love, Grandpa Glen

This is a Bible story book that Glen's father-in-law, as a young boy, got from his grandpa.

Chapter 29 – Sharing the Faith

My father-in-law was not a religious man. He had gone to church and Sunday school as a child but left it behind as a teen. He regarded church as a scam that was after his money. I had a hard time talking to anyone about my faith. It was harder yet with my father-in-law.

As I mentioned earlier, God sometimes leads me through a quiet inner voice that grows in intensity and conviction, especially when I'm fighting it. I experienced this again when Diana and I were staying at Davison (Diana's home town) for a few days. Her dad's drastically declining health had put him in and out of the hospital several times, a pattern that continued the rest of his life. Now he was out.

I felt the Lord's leading to have a serious spiritual discussion with my father-in-law. I declined. I decided instead to go home for a few days. Maybe I would talk to my father-in-law later. I borrowed his car—Diana was staying and would keep ours.

I drove to a gas station and filled the tank. Then I went to the air pump to fill the tires. Suddenly, I had the worst headache of my life. I sat down and recovered a bit before slowly heading back to my in-laws—no going home that evening.

Diana called my brother Ross, the doctor we always turn to for medical advice. He said the symptoms suggested a brain aneurism, a deadly possibility. We called an ambulance and I was rushed to a Flint hospital. They ran a bunch of tests and scans but found nothing. The pain subsided and I was discharged.

The next day, Diana and her mother went shopping. My father-in-law and I were home alone, and my sense that I needed to talk to him about spiritual things was stronger than ever. I wasn't going to ignore it again.

I sat with my father-in-law and shared several stories about my life. I told him that God sometimes speaks to me through a quiet and growing conviction. I told him that I'm a bad listener and often disregard these promptings. I told the story about the first time I went back to church as a young man. I told the story about entering a career in computers when I wanted to stay a janitor. I told about the aneurism scare and that God had been urging me to have this talk with him.

He listened respectfully. I don't know if it registered or if he took it to heart. I do know that I did what I needed to do. I've so often been like Jonah, running the other direction when God tells me to do something. Yet, through all these times, I also see God leading me in a gentle and persistent manner, just as He did with Jonah.

I had another lesson about God working through unlikely circumstances and people. My father had poor social skills that could easily be offensive and embarrassing. He had a hard time seeing another person's perspective. Yet, my dad taught me something valuable—ten years after his death.

A "Pastor Joe" from a church in southern Michigan used Facebook to reach out to my brothers and me. I didn't know him and brushed it off. My brother Ross, who always ignores these things, responded. Joe told Ross that he had searched out our dad's 10-year-old obituary online. Joe was trying to reach the children of Stan Van Antwerp about a man named Wayne who was dying of cancer.

Apparently, Wayne had camped on Van Antwerp family property, next to the Manistee National Forest, over the Memorial Day Weekend in 1986. Pastor Joe told us that Stan, my father and the landowner, had confronted Wayne about being on private land. Stan gave Wayne permission to stay but also gave him a Gideon Bible, a pocket New Testament, that he was carrying. It had Stan Van Antwerp's name inside the cover.

I was dumbfounded to hear this story. I had been there when it happened and had walked over with my dad, standing there as he talked to Wayne.

This New Testament was instrumental in Wayne's walk of faith. He kept it, studied it, and treasured it. My father and Wayne never had any other contact beyond this brief and passing incident. Now Pastor Joe wanted to share Wayne's story at church. He also wanted to project a picture of my dad if we could send something. We scrambled to find a suitable picture. My brother, Bruce, also made arrangements to attend that Sunday service.

Wayne was too sick to attend church that day, but his wife Becky was there. Bruce sat with her during the luncheon that followed the service. Becky told Bruce how Wayne loved to hike, camp, and travel across the Upper Peninsula. She also mentioned that they had purchased a carved hummingbird in Copper Harbor decades earlier. They loved it, but it had finally broken beyond repair.

Bruce told her that his brother, Glen, made that very bird. Then he got her contact info and sent it to me. It took another week before Becky and I actually connected, and she told me that Wayne was now in hospice—fading fast. I told her I'd hurry with a bird.

It was an off week from my own chemotherapy and I felt good. I managed to carve, spread, and dye a hummingbird. It dried overnight. I added several coats of varnish and painted the remaining details. Then I packed and shipped it, including a note that this was a gift from my family to theirs. Becky hung it above Wayne's bed the day it arrived. It was there when he passed away that night, surrounded by the love of God and family.

I'm learning to be more open about my faith. If God could use my father, He could even use me.

A hummingbird like Glen made for Wayne and his family.

Dear Grandkids,

I've always loved hunting. I enjoy being in the woods.

Hunting adds an extra dimension to that experience. The hunter sees the woods more thoroughly and intensely while watching for game.

Hunting is also an enjoyable activity for friends and family. Special bonds form when people hunt together. Getting pure organic meat from a successful hunt is an added bonus.

Here's a few of my hunting stories.

Love, Grandpa Glen

Glen with a buck at the Willow Street house.

Chapter 30 – Hunting

My friend Jeff has always been, and still is, a much better hunter than I am. He prepares more thoroughly, spends more time hunting, and learns from his mistakes. Me, not so much.

Turkey hunting in Northern Michigan grew in popularity during the mid-1970s. Jeff proposed that we should both apply for a spring hunt in Osceola County. I agreed, and we were pleased when our permits came.

Jeff read about turkey hunting, attended seminars, bought various turkey calls, and practiced them faithfully. Turkey season came and we drove north to stay overnight before opening morning. We stopped at a sporting goods store on the way so I could buy a call. I practiced a little as Jeff drove. "That's better," he finally said. "Not too bad."

Next morning's first light found us driving down the two-track at my family property next to the Manistee National Forest. As we stopped the car and got out, a turkey, or what we took for a turkey, called nearby. Then a car came toward us on the two-track which was neither posted nor gated then. An older gentleman stopped and got out.

"This is private property," I informed him. "We're hunting here. I hope you aren't planning on it."

"No," he answered. "I didn't get a permit this year. I was just trying my call to see if any turkeys would answer."

"Did you hear any?"

He cupped his hand to his ear and asked me to repeat the question. The answer was no. We moved our car to let him out, then parked on the track to block other vehicles.

"Let's walk in a bit and set up at a likely place," Jeff suggested. "Then we'll try our calls."

We found a spot and hunkered down. Jeff did a nice gobble and turkeys answered from every direction. These were the real thing, not some old guy trying his call. "Let me quietly slip away," I told Jeff. "You call these guys in."

I moved several hundred yards to a pine-covered hill and hid behind an old stump. I could barely hear turkeys responding to Jeff's call as he tried to coax them in. I pulled out my own call and gave a tentative gobble. Immediately, a tom answered from the bottom of the hill. I watched it strut into a sunlit opening, wings and tail spread wide.

Carefully, quietly, I raised my shotgun and aimed. I hit the bird in the head, a perfect shot. All gobbling ceased when my gun went off, and Jeff never saw a bird.

The tom was huge and delicious when we ate it later. If you've ever eaten properly-cooked wild turkey, you wonder how factory-raised birds get away with their pale imitation. I had the same reaction to this success as I had with the big pike at Cran Hill. I had bagged the trophy of a lifetime and never hunted turkey again.

Another time, I persuaded Diana to go deer hunting with me. I enjoyed it so much and wanted to share the experience. We drove to my uncle's farm west of

Lansing on opening day. We planned to hunt in the woods beyond a field opposite their house.

Snow was falling soft and thick as we walked in. I placed Diana on a stump and told her to keep still. I would move on a couple hundred yards and would come to help if I heard her shoot. I had a great morning. I didn't see a buck, but a little fawn, unaware of my presence, frolicked nearby for half an hour.

After a couple hours, I decided to check on Diana. I found her sitting perfectly still with snow drifted into her lap and covering her gun. I had told her not to move, and she had taken me very literally. She hadn't seen a thing.

"Let's walk up to the house for coffee," I suggested. "You need to warm up."

She agreed and we started out. Approaching the field, I whispered, "Watch carefully, we might see a deer near the edge."

I stalked quietly forward, thinking she was right behind me. I spotted a deer in the field close to the woods. The snow fell thickly and the wind blew my scent away; the deer was unaware of my presence. I turned to see if Diana saw it too, but she was twenty yards behind.

I snuck back and excitedly told her, "There's a deer in the field!"

She asked, "Is it a buck?"

"I don't know, I'll check."

I snuck forward again and saw antlers, a nice six-point set. I turned to see if Diana saw it. She was still twenty yards back. I snuck back again and excitedly told her, "Yes, it's a buck!"

"Why don't you shoot it?" she asked in dumbfounded wonder.

"I didn't think of it", I answered. "I wanted you to see it."

"I stayed back so you could shoot. Go do it."

I crept forward a third time and raised my gun. This time the buck finally glimpsed me and faded back into the woods as I eased my way toward the open field.

Boom! I had driven the buck straight to a neighbor kid who was sitting there. I went over and admired his dead deer, the buck that should have been mine. To add insult to injury, this was his first deer. He had no rope, no knife, and no clue. I field dressed his deer for him and helped him drag it home.

That was the first and last time that Diana went hunting with me. She thought I might do better on my own.

Years later, Jeremy turned fourteen, the minimum age to buy a deer license. We got him equipped and headed to my uncle's on opening morning. Jeremy was slow that day and we were running late. It was already daylight when we reached the woods.

I took Jeremy to a well-used deer trail on the edge of the forest. "Stand here," I whispered as I turned to leave. I hadn't gone twenty yards when I heard a deer approaching. I stopped short and saw a splendid buck, the deer of a lifetime, approaching Jeremy in the first minute of his first deer season. I couldn't do anything but watch. Jeremy stood directly between me and the deer.

The deer stopped and stared. Deer are color blind and couldn't see what was wrong. To him we were out-of-place trees. Jeremy slowly, slowly raised his gun. I had told him that deer don't notice movement if it is slow enough. Jeremy did a perfect job and brought the gun to his shoulder. The deer still stared.

Jeremy aimed and aimed and aimed. The more he aimed, the more the gun wobbled. Then the deer snorted. Jeremy jumped, fired, and missed a deer standing fifteen yards away.

The deer ran off and went straight to where my friend Jeff was sitting. He bagged the biggest buck he'd ever seen.

Several days later, on a gray and misty morning, Jeremy was walking through a field of tall dead goldenrod. A deer that was lying down in the field bounded up and away in twenty-foot leaps. Jeremy swung instinctively and shot it out of the air.

"There's your secret," I teased him. "Next time you see a big buck standing still, make it run so you can hit it."

My friend Blake also hunted with us. He was as colorblind as any deer. He once shot a buck but thought he'd missed. I led him down the deer trail, pointing at each bright-red blood splotch on the ground. To him it was just another brown leaf. We quickly found the dead deer as I teased him about not being able to track a wounded elephant in deep snow.

He got back at me when he shot another buck some years later. It dropped in its tracks, but he waited until I approached. He knew that I would hear his shot and stop by to check. I readied my usual string of insults as I approached. "I think I hit a deer," he said, "but I don't know where it went."

"No, of course you don't."

Then he pointed to the dead deer at his feet and said, "Oh, there it is."

On another occasion, Blake and I and several other hunters were preparing to hunt my property on opening morning. We discussed where we wanted to sit. The home farm was full of deer sign and everybody chose a different corner. There was no place left for Blake and me.

"We'll go up to the other property by the national forest," I volunteered.

"Why did you do that?" Blake stewed as we drove. "It's your property. You deserve first choice."

"Sometimes," I answered, "the best place isn't the best place."

We went different directions when we reached the property and found likely places to sit. By mid-morning we each had a buck and headed home. All the others were skunked.

My grandson James, told me that he wanted to bring a college friend up to hunt during the 2019 deer season. James hadn't previously shown an interest in hunting.

I was delighted and bought a tent blind to set up in a likely place.

I hunted nearby, following my usual hunting technique. I walked slowly and carefully, taking long pauses to stand still at likely spots. I often see deer before they see me, even if I'm walking.

I stopped and stood where several deer trails converge, watching for activity. A deer appeared eighty yards ahead, walking parallel to where I stood. It was partly hidden by trees but walking toward a clearing. I waited and watched.

A good hunter, a hunter like Jeff, would have raised his rifle and followed the deer with his scope. As soon as the deer reached the clearing, he would have squeezed off a shot if the deer looked good. I wasn't a good hunter. I stood still until a big buck stepped into the opening. Then, I quickly raised my gun and fired too rapidly. I missed completely.

I've shot a lot of deer over the years but have never gotten the buck of a lifetime. Perhaps that's why I still hunt.

Dear Grandkids,

Cancer and cancer treatments have monopolized my life for two and a half years. It has been a difficult time.

It has also been a time of great blessing as friends and family have supported us with prayers and love.

Blessings or not, I hope you never get cancer.

Love Grandpa Glen

Flying home from Alaska.

Chapter 31 – Finishing Well

Late in the summer of 2017, I suspected I had a bowel blockage. Something didn't seem right. I made an appointment with my family doctor and got a referral for a colonoscopy. Most people have this checkup every ten years. I was on a five-year schedule because of cancer in my family. I wasn't quite due for another checkup but felt I needed it.

I waited a few days for the referral to go through before calling the surgeon's office. The receptionist asked, "This is your normal five-year checkup, right?"

"No, I suspect something's wrong."

"Well, I can schedule a consult with the doctor in six weeks."

"That's a long time," I said. "Do you have anything sooner?"

"You can see a Physician Assistant at 8:30 tomorrow morning."

"I'll take it!"

The next morning, I described my concerns to the PA. He looked at my records and said, "You've always had clean colonoscopies, not even a hint of a polyp. It's probably nothing serious."

"I understand," I answered. "Still, I want to be checked."

He agreed, checked the computer, and said, "We can schedule you for five weeks from today. You'll have the same doctor as last time."

"That's a long time. Do you have anything sooner?"

"We have a brand-new surgeon starting next week. Will next week work?"

"Yes! I'll take it."

The following week, all prepped and waiting for the doctor, I told the nurses that their anesthesia might not affect me like most people. I told them about my first colonoscopy—fifteen years earlier—when I was their information systems support person. Immediately after my procedure, still under anesthesia, I fixed a problem with their computer program before going home. The nurses chuckled at my story.

The doctor came in and introduced himself. He asked if he could pray with me before starting. I happily agreed. Then I had my anesthesia and we were underway. Midway through the procedure he said, "I've encountered a large mass."

"How large a mass?" I asked.

Taken aback, he answered, "We'll discuss it later."

When he was done and Diana had joined us, he said, "You have a fair-sized tumor that looks like cancer. I'll send a sample to pathology to check for sure."

Pathology reports confirmed his suspicion. Soon, a CT scan showed that the cancer had already spread to a dozen spots in my lungs and liver. The tumor board (a multi-disciplinary group that reviews cases) recommended an immediate start to chemotherapy. My surgeon quickly worked me into his schedule and inserted a port for chemo. He also removed most of the primary tumor in order to get more pathology samples. We were checking to see if I might qualify for a clinical trial at the University of Michigan.

My tumor wasn't the right kind for that trial, so I would get treatments close to home in Cadillac. My oncologist was very frank. He explained that my stage 4 cancer could be treated but not cured. My odds were not good—about a fifty-percent chance of living two and a half years and a ten-percent chance of living five. It was sobering news.

But chemotherapy worked well. Scans and tests at Christmas time showed the cancer in fast retreat. We were very encouraged. As treatment continued, other problems cropped up. I had never been hospitalized before, but now my whole system was weak. I spent several days in the hospital with pneumonia, influenza, and sepsis. Another time I had dangerous blood clots that brought me back to the hospital. Each incident could have been fatal, but I always pulled through.

Eventually, all my cancers disappeared except for the largest of my liver tumors. It grew smaller but never went away. I checked with an Interventional Radiologist in Grand Rapids to see if he could treat the remaining tumor somehow. He took my case to his tumor board.

The Grand Rapids tumor board came back with the shocking and surprising recommendation that I have half my liver removed. It would be a major surgery instead of a small, easy procedure. We discussed it with our family doctor. "This is good news," she said. "They're going for a cure and not just a treatment."

We decided to go for it. First, I had a small operation that encouraged growth in the left liver lobe—the part that would remain. Then, after adequate growth, I had a big operation to remove the right lobe. Hospital recovery in Grand Rapids took a week and a half.

Shortly after discharge, I had complications and went back. One of the nurses walked into my room and said, "Oh good, Glen's back."

"Don't say that," Diana exclaimed. "We don't want to be back."

"I didn't mean it like that," the nurse apologized, "but Glen's a good patient—not everybody is."

After recovery from surgery, the surgeon said I could stay off chemotherapy. He said that any recurring lung tumors could be treated with radiation or surgery. My cancer doctor at home had a different opinion. He wanted me back on chemo immediately. He wanted to be proactive even though I showed no evidence of disease. Tumors too small to see could still be floating around.

I agreed with his assessment and started chemo again. Scans and tests kept coming back clear. After six months, my doctor let me take a break. My summer would be treatment free before we checked again in the fall.

It was a wonderful summer without every-other-week chemo. I was healthy and strong. Steve and I hiked some marvelous miles on the North Country Trail in Michigan's western Upper Peninsula. Diana and I joined good friends on a trip to Alaska. My hair grew back. I didn't look or feel like a cancer patient. I hoped this time would last and last.

It didn't. My next scan showed five tumors scattered all over my lungs. I contacted the surgeon in Grand Rapids, hoping he had options for me. He took my case to his tumor board again. They reviewed it and recommended chemotherapy. The tumors were too many and too scattered to address any other way.

I went back on chemo and my most recent scan looks promising. Still, my future remains uncertain. Cancer is an odd disease. If I had heart trouble, people would tell me how sorry they were. If I had dementia, people would tell my wife how sorry they were.

With cancer, people aren't just sorry, they're hopeful and helpful. Everybody knows an unknown cure that I should try. I'm skeptical. Cancer isn't a single disease. There are many kinds of cancers and many kinds of patients. The likelihood of one miracle cure is small.

When I was a young man, running races, I wanted to finish well. It wasn't enough to have a good start. It wasn't enough to last through the middle. The most important part was to stay strong at the end. Now I'm an old man running a different race. I want to finish strong.

For me, finishing strong means being filled with gratitude. I am immensely thankful for my whole life. Even this cancer experience has brought out the best in my friends and family.

For me, finishing strong means being filled with joy. Each day is a delight, even the worst of my treatment days. I want to enjoy every day that I have.

For me, finishing strong means accepting that I'll die of something, sometime. Everybody does, and many ways of dying are way worse than cancer. It's not as bad as it could be.

For me, finishing strong means living in faith. God has guided and protected me all my days. I could have died in a climbing accident but didn't. I could have died in a car crash but didn't. I could have died falling down a mountain but didn't. I could have perished from an aneurism or a blood clot but didn't. Whenever and however I die, it will be under God's timing and under His care.

For me, finishing strong means finishing this book. I always thought I might write something someday, but someday never came. I am incredibly grateful that I can leave a record of my life. I'm still running life's race with my head high and my spirits strong. The finish line draws nearer.

Acknowledgements:

I extend special thanks to Ben Kilpela and Loraine Meier, much better writers than I, for their early and perceptive suggestions.

The hiking chapters are drawn largely from articles originally published in the "North Star," the North Country Trail Association's magazine.

I also owe endless gratitude to my wife Diana, always my best and truest editor.